S0-AWB-341

DISCARD

THE HOME UNIVERSITY LIBRARY
OF MODERN KNOWLEDGE

CIII

MILTON

MILTON

JOHN BAILEY

FOLCROFT LIBRARY EDITIONS / 1973

Library of Congress Cataloging in Publication Data

Bailey, John Cann, 1864-1931.
  Milton.

  Reprint of the 1915 ed. published by Williams and
Norgate, London.
  Bibliography: p.
  1. Milton, John, 1608-1674.
PR3581.B3 1973   821'.4   73-12210
ISBN 0-8414-3218-X (lib. bdg.)

Limited 100 Copies

Manufactured in the United States of America.

Folcroft Library Editions
Box 182
Folcroft, Pa. 19032

MILTON

JOHN BAILEY

OXFORD UNIVERSITY PRESS
LONDON   NEW YORK   TORONTO

First published in 1915 *and reprinted in* 1923, 1927, 1930, 1932, 1942 *and* 1945

PRINTED IN GREAT BRITAIN

CONTENTS

CHAP.   PAGE

 I INTRODUCTORY 7

 II MILTON'S LIFE AND CHARACTER . . 23

 III THE EARLIER POEMS 89

 IV *PARADISE LOST* 142

 V *PARADISE REGAINED* AND *SAMSON AGO-
   NISTES* 196

  BIBLIOGRAPHY 251

  INDEX 255

v

NOTE TO FOURTH IMPRESSION

See pages 49 and 52

The late Mr. J. S. Smart, Lecturer in English Literature in the University of Glasgow, and author of a scholarly edition of the Sonnets of Milton, believed that Milton's marriage took place in 1642 and not in 1643. The date 1643 has, it seems, no evidence except that of tradition in its favour. Unfortunately, as I am informed by Mr. Peter Alexander, Mr. Smart's successor in the Lectureship, and by Mr. Bernard Wright of the same University, nothing has been found among Mr. Smart's papers dealing with this matter. His belief is known only by memories of conversations held with him by Mr. Alexander and others. But no Miltonic scholar was of higher authority, and he is certain not to have formed his opinion without good reasons. One of them is known to have been the extreme difficulty of getting from London to Oxford in the Spring of 1643 when Oxford was in the hands of the Royal Army. Moreover, the Parliamentary authorities in London allowed no one to go to Oxford without a permit, and Milton's name does not occur on the list, which is extant, of those who received permits. The question of the date is not unimportant, for, if Mr. Smart was right and the marriage really took place in 1642, Masson's ugly suspicion that Milton began his first divorce pamphlet before his wife left him falls to the ground. The little that is known on this matter was set out by M. Denis Saurat, who had discussed it with Mr. Smart, in an article printed in the *Revue Anglo-Américaine* for August 1925. I owe this reference to the kindness of Mr. Bernard Wright.

I may add here that with another accusation against Milton never believed by anyone who in the least understood his character Mr. Smart dealt conclusively in a posthumous article, 'Milton and the King's Prayer,' published in *The Review of English Studies* for October 1925.

MILTON

CHAPTER I

INTRODUCTORY

WHEN a man spends a day walking in hilly country he is often astonished at the new shape taken on by a mountain when it is looked at from a new point of view. Sometimes the change is so great as to make it almost unrecognizable. He who has seen Snowdon from Capel-Curig is reluctant to admit that what he sees from Llanberis is the same mountain : he who has seen the Langdale Pikes from Glaramara is amazed at their beauty as he gazes at them from the garden at Low Wood. These are extreme cases. But to a less degree every traveller among the mountains is experiencing the same thing all day. He finds the eternal hills the most plastic of forms. At each change in his own position there is a change in the shape of a mountain under which he is passing. He may keep his eye fixed upon it but insensibly, as he watches, the long

7

chain will become a vertical peak, the jagged
precipice a round green slope.

Much the same process goes on as the
generations of men pass on their way, with
their eyes fixed, as they cannot help being,
on the great human heights of their own and
earlier days. Many of these look great only
when you are close to them. At a little
distance they are seen to be small and soon
they disappear altogether. The true mountains remain but they do not keep the same
shape. Each succeeding generation sees the
peaks of humanity from a new point of view
which cannot be exactly the same as that of
its predecessor. Each age reshapes for itself
its conception of art, of poetry, of religion, and
of human life which includes them all. Of
some of the masters in each of these worlds
it feels that they belong not to their own
generation only but to all time and so to
itself. It cannot be satisfied, therefore, with
what its predecessors have said about them.
It needs to see them again freshly for itself,
and put into words so far as it can its own
attitude towards them.

That is the excuse for the new books which
will always be written every few years about
Hebrew Religion, or Greek Art, or the French
Revolution, or about such men as Plato,

St. Paul, Shakspeare, Napoleon. It is the
excuse even for a much humbler thing, for
the addition of a volume on Milton to the
Home University Library. The object of
this Library is not, indeed, to say anything
startlingly new about the great men with
whom it deals. Rather the contrary, in
fact : for to say anything startlingly new
about Shakspeare or Plato would probably
be merely to say what is absurd or false.
The main outlines of these great figures have
long been settled, and the man who writes
a book to prove that Shakspeare was not a
great dramatist, or was an exact and lucid
writer, is wasting his own time and that of
his readers. The mountain may change its
aspect from hour to hour, but when once we
have ascertained that it is composed of
granite, that matter is settled, and there is
no use in arguing that it is sandstone or
basalt. The object of such volumes as those
of this Library is no vain assault on the
secure judgment-seat of the world, no hopeless appeal against the recorded and accepted
decrees of time. It is rather to re-state
those decrees in modern language and from
the point of view of our own day : to show,
for instance, how Plato, though no longer for
us what he was for the Neo-Platonists, is

A 2

still for us the most moving mind of the
race that more than all others has moved
the mind of the world; how Milton, though
no longer for us a convincing justifier of the
ways of God to men, is still a figure of tran-
scendent interest, the most lion-hearted, the
loftiest-souled, of Englishmen, the one consummate artist our race has produced, the
only English man of letters who in all that
is known about him, his life, his character,
his poetry, shows something for which the
only fit word is sublime.

There was much else beside, of course.
The sublime is very near the terrible, and
the terrible is often not very far removed
from the hateful. Dante giving his " daily
dreadful line " to the private and public
enemies with whom he grimly populates his
hell is not exactly an amiable or attractive
figure. Still less so is Milton in those prose
pamphlets in which he passes so rapidly,
and to us so strangely, from the heights of
heaven to the gutter mud of scurrilous personalities. This is a disease from which our
more amiable age seems at last to have
delivered the world. But Milton has at
least the excuse of a long and august tradition,
from the days of Demosthenes, equally profuse
of a patriotism as lofty and of personalities as

base as Milton's, to those of a whole line of
the scholars of the Renaissance who lived
with the noblest literature of the world and
wrote of each other in the language of Billings-
gate fishwives. So the sublimity of his life
is wholly that of an irresistible will, set from
the first on achieving great deeds and
victoriously achieving them in defiance of
adverse men and fates. But this is quite
compatible with qualities the reverse of
agreeable. It is the business of sublimity
to compel amazed admiration, not to be a
pleasant companion. Milton rejoicing over
the tortures bishops will suffer in hell, Milton
insulting Charles I, Milton playing the tyrant
to his daughters, none of these are pleasant
pictures. But such incidents, if perhaps
unusually grim in the case of Milton, are
apt to happen with Olympians. Experience
shows that it is generally best to listen to
their thunder from a certain distance.

Such limitations must not be ignored.
But neither must they be unduly pressed.
The important thing about the sun is not its
spots but its light and heat. No great poet
in all history, with the possible exception of
Dante, has so much heat as Milton. In prose
and verse alike he burns and glows with fire.
At its worst it is a fire of anger and pride, at

its best a fire of faith in liberty, justice, righteousness, God. Of the highest of all fires, the white flame of love, it has indeed little. Milton had no Beatrice to teach him how to show men the loveliness of the divine law, the beauty of holiness. He could describe the loss of Paradise and even its recovery, but its eternal bliss, the bliss of those who live in the presence of

l'amor che move il sole e l'altre stelle,

he could not describe. To do that required one who had seen the Vita Nuova before he saw the Inferno. *In la sua volontade è nostra pace.* So Dante thought : but not altogether so Milton. It is not a difference of theological opinion : it is a difference of temper. For Dante the " will of God " at once suggested both the apostolic and the apocalyptic love, joy, peace, the supreme and ultimate beatific vision. Bitter as his life on earth had been, no man ever suffering more from evil days and evil tongues, no man ever more bitterly conscious of living in an evil and perverse generation, he had yet within him a perpetual fountain of peace in the thought of God's will, and the faith that he was daily advancing nearer to the light of heaven and the divine presence. Milton, a sincere believer in God

if man ever were, must also at times have
had his moments of beatific vision in which
the invisible peace of God became more real
than the storms of earthly life and the vile-
ness of men. Indeed, we see the traces of
such moments in the opening of *Comus*, in
the concluding lines of *Lycidas*, in the sustained ecstasy of *At a Solemn Music*. But
they appear to have been only moments.
Milton was a lifelong Crusader who scarcely
set foot in the Holy Land. The will of God
meant for him not so much peace as war.
He is a prophet rather than a psalmist.
" Woe is me, my Mother, that thou hast born
me a man of strife and contention," he
himself complains in the *Reason of Church
Government*. He was not much over thirty
when he wrote those words : and they remained true of him to the end. For twenty
years the strife was active and public; ever,
in appearance at least, more and more successful : then for the final fourteen it became
the impotent wrath of a caged and wounded
lion. Never for a moment did his soul bow
to the triumph of the idolaters : but neither
could it forget them, nor make any permanent
escape into purer air. *Paradise Lost, Paradise
Regained* and *Samson*, especially the last, are
all plainly the works of a man conscious of

having been defeated by a world which he could defy but could not forget. Sublimely certain of the righteousness of his cause, he has no abiding certainty of its victory. He hears too plainly the insulting voices of the sons of Belial, and broods in proud and angry gloom over the ruin of all his hopes, personal, political and ecclesiastical. And as his religion was a thing of intellect and conscience, not a thing of spiritual vision, he cannot make for himself that mystical trans-valuation of all earthly doings in the light of which the struggles of political and ecclesiastical parties are seen as things temporary, trivial and of little account.

Such are the limitations of Milton. They are those of a man who lived in the time of a great national struggle, deliberately chose his own side in it, and from thenceforth saw nothing in the other but folly, obstinacy and crime. He has in him nothing whatever of the universal, and universally sympathetic, insight of Shakspeare. And he has paid the price of his narrowness in the open dislike, or at best grudging recognition, of that half of the world which is not Puritan and not Republican, and still looks upon history, custom, law and loyalty with very different eyes from his. But those who exact that penalty do themselves at least as much injustice as they do Milton. To deprive ourselves of Milton because we are neither Puritan moralists nor Old Testament politicians is an act of intellectual suicide. The wise, as the world goes on, may differ more and more from some of Milton's opinions. They can never escape the greatness either of the poet or of the man. Men's appreciation of Milton is almost in proportion to their instinctive understanding of what greatness is. Other poets, perhaps, have things of greater beauty : none in English, none, perhaps, in any language, fills us with a more exalting conviction of the greatness of human life. No man rises from an hour with Milton without feeling ashamed of the triviality of his life and certain that he can, if he will, make it less trivial. It is impossible not to catch from him some sense of the high issues, immediate and eternal, on 'which human existence ought to be conscious that it hangs. The world will be very old before we can spare a man who can render us this service. We have no one in England who renders it so imperiously as Milton.

This part of his permanent claim upon our attention belongs to all that we know of him, to everything in his life so far as it is recorded

even to his prose, where its appearances are
occasional, as well as to his verse, where it is
continuous and omnipresent.   It is, of course,
in connection with the last that we are most
conscious of it and that it is most important.
After all, the rest would have been unknown
or forgotten if he had not been a great poet.
But it is not merely by his force of mind and
character, nor merely by the influence they
have upon us through the poetry, that he
claims our attention to-day.   Altogether in-
dependently of that, the study of Milton is
of immense and special value to Englishmen.
Except in poetry our English contribution to
the life of the arts in Europe has been comparatively small.   That very Puritanism which
had so much to do with the greatness of
Milton has also had much to do with the
general failure of Englishmen to produce
fine art, or even to care about it, or so much
as recognize it when they see it.   Now Milton,
Puritan as he was, was always, and not least
in his final Puritan phase, a supreme artist.
Poetry has been by far our greatest artistic
achievement and he is by far our greatest
poetic artist.   No artist in any other field,
no Inigo Jones or Wren, no Purcell, no
Reynolds or Turner, holds such unquestioned
eminence in any other art as he in his.   If

the world asks us where to look for the genius
of England, so far as it has ever been expressed on paper, we point, of course, un-
hesitatingly to Shakspeare. But Shakspeare
is as inferior to Milton in art as he is superior
in genius. His genius will often, indeed,
supply the place of art; but the possession of
powers that are above art is not the same
thing as being continuously and consciously
a great artist. We can all think of many
places in his works where for hundreds of
lines the most censorious criticism can scarcely
wish a word changed; but we can also think
of many in which the least watchful cannot
fail to wish much changed and much omitted.
" Would he had blotted a thousand " is still
a true saying, and its truth known and felt
by all but the blindest of the idolaters of
Shakspeare. No one has ever uttered such
a wish about the poetry of Milton. This is
not the place to anticipate a discussion of
it which must come later. But, in an introductory chapter which aims at insisting upon
the present and permanent importance of
Milton, it is in place to point out the immense
value to the English race of acquaintance
with work so conscientiously perfect as
Milton's. English writers on the whole have
had a tendency to be rather slipshod in

expression and rather indifferent to the finer
harmonies of human speech, whether as a
thing of pure sound or as a thing of sounds
which have more than mere meaning, which
have associations. Milton as both a lover of
music and a scholar is never for a moment
unconscious of either. It would scarcely be
going too far to say that there is not a word
in his verse which owes its place solely to the
fact that it expresses his meaning. All the
words accepted by his instinctive or deliberate
choice were accepted because they provided
him with the most he could obtain of three
qualities which he desired : the exact expression of the meaning needed for the immediate
purpose in hand, the associations fittest to
enhance or enrich that meaning, the rhythmical
or musical effect required for the verse. The
study of his verse is one that never exhausts
itself, so that the appreciation of it has been
called the last reward of consummate scholarship. But the phrase does Milton some injustice. It is true that the scholar tastes
again and again in Milton some flavour of
association or suggestion which is not to be
perceived by those who are not scholars, and
it is also true that he consciously understands
what he is enjoying more than they possibly
can. But neither Milton's nor any other

great art makes its main appeal to learning.
What does that is not art at all but pedantry.
Those who have never read a line of the Greek
and Latin poets certainly miss many pleasures
in reading Milton, but, if they have any ear for
poetry at all, they do not miss either the mind
or the art of Milton.   The unconquerable will,
the high soaring soul, are everywhere audibly
present : and so, even to those who have little
reading and no knowledge at all of matters
of rhythm or metre, are the grave Dorian
music, the stately verses rolling in each after
the other like great ocean waves in eternal
difference, in eternal sameness.   The ignorant
ear hears and rejoices, with a delight that
passes understanding, as the ignorant eye sees
a fine drawing or a piece of Greek sculpture
and without understanding enjoys, learns, and
unconsciously grows in keenness of sight.   To
live with Milton is necessarily to learn that
the art of poetry is no triviality, no mere
amusement, but a high and grave thing, a
thing of the choicest discipline of phrase, the
finest craftsmanship of structure, the most
nobly ordered music of sound.   The ordinary
reader may not be conscious of any such
lessons :   but he learns them nevertheless.
And from no one else in English can he learn
them so well as from Milton.

For these reasons, these and others, we must cling to our great epic poet, Shelley's "third among the sons of light." He is not easy reading : the greatest seldom are : but as with all the greatest, each new reading is not only easier than the last but fuller of matter for thought, wonder and delight. At each new reading, too, the things in him that belonged to his own age, the Biblical literalism, the theological prepossessions, the political partisanship, recede more and more into the background and leave us freer to enjoy the things which belong to all time. And to all peoples. Milton is, indeed, intensely English and could not have been anything but an Englishman. His profound conviction of the greatness of moral issues, and his passionate love of liberty, have both been characteristic of the Englishmen of whom England is most proud. Till lately too, at any rate, we should have said that his fierce individualism, intellectual and political, was English too. But his mind and soul, stored with the gathered riches of many languages and of an inward experience far too intense to be confined by national limitations, reach out to a world wider altogether than this island, wider even than Europe. In *Samson Agonistes* it is hard to say who is more vividly present, the English politician, the Greek tragedian, or the Hebrew prophet. And in one sense *Paradise Lost* is the most universal of all poems. Indeed, that word may be applied to it in its strictest meaning, for the field of Milton's action is not Greece, or Italy, or England, or even the whole earth; it is the universe itself. That is one of its difficulties: but it is also a source of the uplifting and enlarging quality which is peculiarly Miltonic. With him we are conscious of treading no petty scene. We have in some respects travelled far from Milton's way both of stating and of solving his problem, but nevertheless it is still with us to-day and always: the problem of man's origin and destiny, of the ways of God to men. And though Milton is more hampered by literal belief in a particular theological legend than the authors of the *Book of Job* and the *Prometheus Vinctus*, yet, like these, he shows that a great mind and soul will leave the imprint of power and truth on the most incredible primitive story. To read his great poem, or indeed any of his poems, is to live for a while in the presence of one of those royal souls, those natural kings of men, whom Plato felt to be born to rule and inspire their fellows: and the heroic temper of the man is in England less rare than the consummate

WHITWORTH COLLEGE LIBRARY
SPOKANE, WASH.

perfection of art which has eternalized its
utterance. This is Milton : and, though we
may be too weak to read him often, we
shall never be able to do without him, never
think of him without an added strength and
exaltation of spirit.

CHAPTER II

WE know far more about Milton than about any other English poet born so long ago. There are three reasons for this. One is that from his earliest years he was very much interested in himself, was quite aware that he was a man above the stature of ordinary men, and had the most deliberate intention and expectation of doing great things. Consequently he is not only, like most good poets, fond of bringing more or less concealed autobiography into his poetry, but still more in his prose works he inclines often to insert long passages about himself, his studies, travels, projects, friends and character. It is these more than anything else which now keep those works alive : and, coming from a man so proudly truthful as Milton evidently was, they are of the greatest interest and value. The second reason why we know so much about him is that he played an active part in politics, a far more certain way of attracting contemporary attention in England than writing *Hamlet* or building St. Paul's Cathedral. And the third is that his life has been made the subject of perhaps the most minute and elaborate biography in the language. Mr. Masson's labours enable us to know, if we choose, every fact, however insignificant, which the most laborious investigation can discover, not only about Milton himself but, one may almost say, about everybody who was ever for five minutes in Milton's company.

From this mass of material, all that can be touched here is a few of the most salient facts of the life and the most striking features of the character.

Milton's life is naturally divided into three periods. The first is that of his education and early poems. It extends from his birth in 1608 to his return from his foreign travels in 1639. The second is that of his political activity, and extends from 1639 to the Restoration. The third is that of *Paradise Lost*, *Paradise Regained* and *Samson*. It concludes with his death, on November 8, 1674.

Milton was born on December 9, 1608, at a house in Bread Street, Cheapside. The house is gone, but the street is a very short one, and it is still pleasant to step out of the

roar of Cheapside into its quietness, and think
that there, on the left, close by, under the
shadow of Bow Church, was born the greatest
poet to whom the greatest city of the modern
world has given birth. London ought to
hold fast to the honour of Milton, for his
honour is peculiarly hers. He was not only
born a Londoner but lived in London nearly
all his life. And his mind is throughout that
of the citizen. Neither agriculture nor sport
means much to him; and, much as he loves
the sights and sounds of the open country,
his allusions to them are those of the delighted
but still wondering alien, not those of the
native. None is more often quoted than the
passage in the ninth book of *Paradise Lost*—

" As one who, long in populous city pent,
  Where houses thick and sewers annoy the
      air,
  Forth issuing on a summer's morn, to
      breathe
  Among the pleasant villages and farms
  Adjoined, from each thing met conceives
      delight—
  The smell of grain, or tedded grass, or kine,
  Or dairy, each rural sight, each rural sound—
  If chance with nymph-like step fair virgin
      pass,
  What pleasing seemed for her now pleases
      more,
  She most, and in her look sums all delight."

And the secret of its charm obviously lies partly in the note of a personal experience. Just in that way must Milton, as boy and man, have often issued forth from the weariness of his studies and the noise and confinement of the streets, for a walk among the open fields that then lay so close at hand for the Londoner. And perhaps, as the inhabitants of towns often do, he took a pleasure in the very hedgerows unknown to those who saw them every day. The present Poet Laureate, who has spent most of his life in the country, has asked a question to which it is not easy for the countryman to give the answer he would like—

> " Whose spirit leaps more high,
> Plucking the pale primrose,
> Than his whose feet must fly
> The pasture where it grows ? "

If the town-dweller never attains to that mystical communion with the secret soul of Nature which Wordsworth and such as Wordsworth owe to a life spent in the " temple's inmost shrine," yet his eye, undulled by familiarity, commonly sees more in trees and flowers than the eyes of nearly all those who live every day among them. At its highest familiarity breeds intimacy, but more often what it breeds is indifference. A man who reads the Bible for the first time in middle life will never live inside it as some saints have lived; but he will see much that is hidden from most of those who have been reading it every day since they could read at all.

Milton remained in London, so far as we know, for the first sixteen years of his life. He was educated at St. Paul's School by a private tutor, one Thomas Young, who was later a conspicuous Presbyterian figure, and by his father, to whom he owed far more than to any one except himself. The elder John Milton was a remarkable man. He had, to begin with, deserted the religious views of his family and taken a line of his own, a course which may not always indicate wisdom, but always indicates force of character. The poet's grandfather, who lived in the Oxford country, had adhered very definitely to Roman Catholicism and is said to have cast off his son for becoming a Protestant and something of a Puritan. The son went to London, set up in business as a scrivener, that is, as something like a modern solicitor, and prospered so much that by 1632 he was able to retire and live in the country. He had considerable musical talents, and his compositions are found in collections of tunes to which such

men as Morley, Dowland and Orlando Gibbons
contributed. His house was no doubt full of
music, as were, indeed, many others in that
most · musical of English centuries, and it
must have been primarily to him that the
poet owed the intense delight in music which
appears in all his works. No poet speaks of
music so often, and none in his poetry so often
suggests that art. The untaught music of
lark or nightingale he has not; but no poet
has so much of the music which is one of the
most consciously elaborate of those arts by
which man expresses at once his senses, his
mind and his soul.

In the spring of 1625, just a month or two
after the accession of the king whose tragical
fate was to be the original source of Milton's
European fame and very nearly the cause
of his mounting a scaffold himself, the future
author of *Paradise Lost* went into residence
at Cambridge where he remained for seven
years. The college that can boast his name
among its members is Christ's. Unlike so
many poets he had a successful university
career, took the ordinary degrees, and
evidently made an impression on his contemporaries. No doubt the strong natural
bias to a studious life which he had from a
child made him apter for university discipline

than is usually the case with genius. From
the beginning he had the passion of the
student. He says of himself that from his
twelfth year he scarce ever went to bed before
midnight; and Aubrey reports much the
same and says that his father " ordered the
maid to sit up for him." And his studies were
in the main the accepted studies of the time,
not, like Shelley's, a defiance of them. All
through his life he had a scholar's respect
for learning, and for the great tradition of
literature which it is the true business of
scholarship to maintain. Radical and rebel
as he was in politics and theology, contemptuous of law, custom and precedent, he was
always the exact opposite in his art. There
he never attempted the method of the *tabula
rasa*, or clean slate, which made his political
pamphlets so barren. The greatest of all
proofs of the strength of his individuality is
that it so entirely dominates the vast store
of learning and association with which his
poetry is loaded. Such a man will at least
give his university a chance; and, though
Milton did not in later life look back on Cambridge with great affection or respect, there
can be no doubt that the seven years he spent
within the walls of a college were far from
useless to the poet who more than any other

was to make learning serve the purposes of
poetry.

So strong, self-reliant and proudly virtuous
a nature was not likely to be altogether
popular either with the authorities or with
his companions. Nor was he, at any rate at
first. He had some difference with his tutor,
had to leave Cambridge for a time, and is
alleged, on very doubtful evidence, to have
been flogged. But, whatever his fault was,
it was nothing that he was ashamed of, for
he publicly alluded to the affair in his Latin
poems, and was never afraid to challenge
inquiry into his Cambridge career. Nor did
it injure him permanently with the authorities.
He took his degrees at the earliest possible
dates, and ten years after he left Cambridge
was able to write publicly and gratefully of
" the more than ordinary respect which I
found, above many of my equals, at the hands
of those courteous and learned men, the
Fellows of that college wherein I spent some
years : who, at my parting after I had taken
two degrees, as the manner is, signified many
ways how much better it would content them
that I would stay : as by many letters full of
kindness and loving respect, both before that
time and long after, I was assured of their
singular good affection towards me." The

Fellows were no doubt clerical dons of the
ordinary sort : indeed, we know they were;
but they could not have Milton among them
for seven years without discovering that he
was something above the ordinary undergraduate. Wood, who died in 1695 and
therefore writes as a contemporary, says of
Milton that while at Cambridge he was
" esteemed to be a virtuous and sober person
yet not to be ignorant of his own parts."
Such young men may not be popular, but
if they have the real thing in them they
soon compel respect.   By the undergraduates
Milton was called " The Lady of Christ's."
And it is plain, from his own references to
this nickname in a Prolusion delivered in the
college, that he owed it not only to his fair
complexion, short stature and great personal
beauty, but also to the purity, delicacy and
refinement of his manners.   He contemptu-
ously asks the audience who had given him
the nickname whether the name of manhood
was to be confined to those who could drain
great tankards of ale or to peasants whose
hands were hard with holding the plough.
He disdains the implied charge of prudery,
and indeed his language is what could not have
been used by an effeminate or a coward.   No
braver man ever held a pen.   Wood says

that "his deportment was affable, his gait erect, bespeaking courage and undauntedness," and he himself tells us that "he did not neglect daily practice with his sword," and that "when armed with it, as he generally was, he was in the habit of thinking himself quite a match for any one and of being perfectly at ease as to any injury that any one could offer him." Evidently he owed his title of "Lady" to no weakness, but to a disgust at the coarse and barbarous amusements then common at the universities. He says of himself that he had no faculty for "festivities and jests," as indeed was to be witnessed by all his writings. The witticisms, if such they can be called, which occur in his poetry and oftener in his prose are akin to what are now called practical jokes, that is jokes made by the bodies of those whose minds are not capable of joking. This was partly the common fault of an age whose jests, as may be seen sometimes even in Shakspeare, appear to us to alternate between the merely obvious, the merely verbal, and the merely barbarous; but it was partly also the peculiar temperament of Milton, whose sense of humour, like that of many learned and serious men, was so sluggish that it could only be moved by a very violent stimulus.

But in the main with Milton there was no
question of jests, good or bad. It is evident
from his own proud confessions that he was
always intensely serious, at least from his
Cambridge days, always conscious of the
greatness of life's issues, always uplifted with
the noblest sort of ambition. He says of
himself that, however he might admire the
art of Ovid and poets of Ovid's sort, he soon
learnt to dislike their morals and turned from
them to the " sublime and pure thoughts " of
Petrarch and Dante. And his " reasonings,
together with a certain niceness of nature, an
honest haughtiness, and self-esteem either of
what I was or what I might be (which let
envy call pride) . . . kept me still above
those low descents of mind beneath which he
must deject and plunge himself that can agree
to saleable and unlawful prostitutions." And
in repudiating an impudently false charge
against his own character he boldly announces
a doctrine far above his own age, one, indeed,
to which ours has not yet attained. " Having
had the doctrine of Holy Scripture unfolding
these chaste and high mysteries with timeliest
care infused that ' the body is for the Lord
and the Lord for the body,' thus also I argued
to myself,—that, if unchastity in a woman,
whom St. Paul terms the glory of man, be

B

such a scandal and dishonour, then certainly
in a man, who is both the image and glory
of God, it must, though commonly not so
thought, be much more deflowering and dis-
honourable. . . . Thus large I have purposely
been that, if I have been justly taxed with
this crime, it may come upon me after all this
my confession with a tenfold shame."

Such was the man from the first, severe
with others and with himself, conscious,
almost from boyhood, in his own famous
words, that " he who would not be frustrate
of his hope to write well hereafter in laudable
things ought himself to be a true poem "; a
somewhat strange figure, no doubt, among the
tavern-haunting undergraduates of the seventeenth century, a stranger still to be honoured,
a hundred and fifty years later, in the rooms
then and now remembered as his, by the
nearest approach to drunkenness in the long
and virtuous life of Wordsworth. When he
left the university in 1632 Milton had con-
quered respect, though probably not popularity.   The tone of the sixth of the academic
Orations, which he delivered at Cambridge
and allowed to be published in his old age,
shows that, being still aware that he was not
popular, he was surprised and pleased at the
applause with which a previous discourse of

his had been received and at the large gather-
ing which had crowded to hear the one he
was delivering. He says that "nearly the
whole flower of the university" was present;
and, after allowing for compliments, it is plain
that only a man whose name aroused expectations could draw an audience which could be
so described without obvious absurdity.

We may well then believe that there is no
great exaggeration in his nephew's statement,
substantially confirmed as it is by other
evidence, that when Milton left Cambridge
in 1632 he was already "loved and admired
by the whole university, particularly by the
Fellows and most ingenious persons of his
House." He had, as Wood says, "performed
the collegiate and academical exercises to the
admiration of all." The power of his mind,
the grave strength of his character, could not
but be plain to all who had come into close
contact with him, and even for those who
had not he was a man who had distinction
plainly written on his face. It is possible,
even, that he was already known as a poet.
Before he left Cambridge he had written
several of the poems which we still read in
his works : the beautiful stanzas *On the Death
of a Fair Infant*, so like and so unlike the
early poems of Shakspeare, the noble *Ode*

on the Nativity begun probably on Christmas
Day 1629, though this is not certain; the
pretty little *Song on May Morning* which
one likes to fancy having been sung at some
such Cambridge greeting of the rising May
Day sun as that which is still performed
on Magdalen Tower at Oxford; certainly
the remarkable lines which are his tribute
to Shakspeare : certainly also the beautiful
Epitaph on the Marchioness of Winchester ;
and, to mention no more, the autobiographical
sonnet on attaining the age of twenty-three.
None of these except the lines on Shakspeare
are known to have been published before
they appeared in the volume of Milton's poems
issued in 1645.   But the fact that those lines
were printed, though without Milton's name,
among the commendatory verses prefixed to
the 1632 Folio Edition of Shakspeare, may
imply that Milton was already known as a
young poet.   There is also a story that the
poem on the death of Lady Winchester was
printed in a contemporary Cambridge collection.   But whether this were so or not (and no
such volume is known to have existed), it seems
almost certain that some of Milton's poems
would have got known by being passed about
in manuscript copies.   He himself from the
first undervalued nothing he wrote, and was

not afraid to say publicly, in his *Reason of Church Government*, that, from his early youth, it had been found that, " whether aught was imposed me by them that had the overlooking, or betaken to of mine own choice in English or other tongue, prosing or versing, but chiefly this latter, the style, by certain signs it had, was likely to live." He published these bold words in 1641, when he had given no public proof at all of their truth. Such a man was not likely to be unwilling that his verses should be seen : and in particular such poems as the epitaph on Lady Winchester, whose death aroused much public interest, or the *Ode on the Nativity*, plainly challenging the greatest of his predecessors by its high theme and noble art, are almost sure to have got about and won him some fame.

He had earned distinction, then, and aroused expectation before the end of his university career. But what surprised his contemporaries was that for the next seven or eight years he appeared to do little or nothing to justify the one or fulfil the other. Leaving Cambridge when he was twenty-three, he entered no profession, but lived till he was past twenty-nine in studious retirement at his father's country house at Horton near Windsor. His father, and other friends, very naturally remonstrated at this apparent inactivity. To them all the answer is the same. He cannot now enter the Church, as he had intended, because he would not " subscribe slave " and take oaths that he could not keep. He is not surrendering himself to " the endless delight of speculation," or to the pleasure of " dreaming away his years in the arms of studious retirement." No; he has other things in view than these : but for their performance he demands time for himself and patience from his friends : his own thought is not of being early or late but of being fit. And the work for which he is preparing is in his own mind a settled thing. It is literature, poetry, and, in particular, as will soon appear more definitely, a great poem to take its place among the great poems of the world.

The writing of poetry has never been a recognized and seldom a lucrative profession. Most poets, like other artists, have had to face family opposition and the danger of poverty in obeying their inward call. In this matter Milton is one of the great exceptions. Many poets have had fathers as rich as his, but it would not be easy to find one who resigned himself so cheerfully to the prospect of having a poetic son. The elder Milton was, however, as we have seen, no ordinary man. His sense

of the value of the things of the mind was
almost as great as his faith in his son and far
greater than his ambition for his son's visible
success in the eyes of the world. He had
naturally hoped that that son's evident
abilities would be exhibited in the ordinary
course in a recognized profession; and he
evidently made some protest against the
apparently objectless studies which, even
after leaving Cambridge, Milton seemed to
regard as his sole business in life. The record
of this survives in the Latin poem *Ad Patrem*
which is plainly a reply to some such remon-
strance. It is an appeal, and one of very
confident tone, to his father not to scorn the
Muses to whom he himself owes his own great
musical gifts. Why should he, a musician, be
astonished to find that his son is a poet?
Poetry more than any of man's other gifts is
the proof of his divine origin : music and
poetry rank together; may it not be that he
and his father have divided between them the
two great gifts of Apollo?

" Dividuumque Deum genitorque puerque
    tenemus."

The poem rings with the scorn of wealth,
from which one must suppose that the old
man of business had pointed out that the

scholar's life was not usually lived under the
smiles of Fortune.   How can you, of all men,
replies his son, ask me to care much for that?
You trained me from the first for learning, not
for the City or the Bar; the father who had
his son taught not only Latin, but Greek and
Hebrew, French and Italian, astronomy and
physical science, cannot ask him to regard
money making as the object of life.   I have
chosen a better part than that : and you were
the inspirer of my choice.   And I know that
at heart you agree with it and share it.

The poem is one of the most interesting
of Milton's Latin poems, being rather less
affected than most of them by that artificiality
of classical allusion which is the bane of such
productions.   So far as we know, it was the
last word on its subject.   From henceforth
no one questioned Milton's right to be a poet
and himself.   If he ever afterwards deserted
his poetic vocation it was at what he believed
to be a still higher call.   For the present he
lived on quietly at Horton, near the Church
where his mother's grave may still be seen;
walking often, as we may suppose, about that
quietly beautiful country washed by the
Thames and crowned by Windsor Castle; and
sometimes, as we know from his own words,
travelling the seventeen or eighteen miles to

London to buy books or learn " anything new
in Mathematics or in Music, in which sciences
I then delighted." Some of these visits to
London evidently lasted days or weeks.

The interesting thing about these six years
at Horton is that they are the only part
of his life during which the least rural of
our poets lived continuously in the country.
And perhaps we may say that they bore
their natural fruit; for it was while he was
at Horton that Milton wrote *L'Allegro* and
Il Penseroso, in which he touched rural life
and rural scenes with a freshness and directness which he never again equalled. And
the most important of the other poems
written during these years, *Arcades*, *Comus*,
and above all, *Lycidas*, show the same influence. *Arcades* and *Comus* point also to
the effect of his visits to London and the
musical world : for both of these were written
for the music of his friend Henry Lawes,
and probably at his suggestion; and, written
as they were for entertainments given by
members of the noble families of Stanley and
Egerton, they show that Milton's plan of life
did not involve cutting himself off from the
great world, where they must have caused
his name to be talked of.   His life at Horton
was evidently not that of a mere recluse,

B 2

forgetting the world outside and forgotten by it. *Arcades* and *Comus*, and still more the wonderful outburst *At a Solemn Music*, are visible links with the cultivated circles of the town, as *Lycidas*, which followed them in 1637 and was printed in 1638 at Cambridge with other poems to the memory of Edward King, is a visible link with his old university.

The mention of the poems of these years, the most delightful that Milton was ever to write, show that the six years spent at Horton were not entirely what he calls them, " a complete holiday spent in reading over the Greek and Latin writers." If he had never written another line, he had written enough by the time he left Horton to give him a place among the very greatest men who have practised the art of poetry in England. When he started abroad in 1638 he must have known, and his father too, that his daring choice had already justified itself. " You ask what I am about, what I am thinking of," he writes to his friend Diodati at the end of the Horton time; " why, with God's help, of immortality." It is the voice of a man who knows he has already done great things but counts them as nothing compared with what he is to do later on.

Man proposes. In 1637 Milton was " plum-

ing his wings " for the very mightiest of poetic
flights, for such a poem as would give full
scope to his genius and place him among the
great poets of the world. But in the result
he actually wrote less poetry in the next
twenty years than he had written in the
previous five : less in quantity and far less
in quality and importance. The first inter-
ruption was the completion of his elaborate
education by a grand tour. His generous
father, who was well-to-do rather than rich,
had acquiesced in his not so far earning one
penny for himself, and was now prepared to
provide him with about a thousand pounds
of our present money to enable him to go
abroad for a year or two in comfortable
style and with the attendance of a servant.
Leaving England in the spring of 1638, he
spent a few days in Paris, where he was
civilly entertained by the famous Grotius,
then Swedish Ambassador there, as well as
by the English Ambassador, Lord Scudamore, but soon moved south, entering Italy
by Nice and Genoa and arriving at Florence
in August or September. There he spent
two months, and was enthusiastically received by the various academies or clubs
of men of letters which then flourished in
Florence, one of whose still existing minute

books records that at its meeting on September the 16th a certain John Milton, an Englishman, read to the members a Latin hexameter poem showing great learning. There also he paid his famous visit to Galileo, now old and blind, and still a sort of nominal prisoner of the Inquisition, for the sin, as Milton says in the *Areopagitica*, of " thinking in Astronomy otherwise than the Franciscan and Dominican licensers thought." One may be sure that it was not merely the interest of the new theory about the motion of the earth which drew him back so often to that question in *Paradise Lost*. The blind astronomer, whose scientific heresies had placed him in some danger of the thumbscrew, must have been a very near and moving memory to the blind poet whose political and ecclesiastical heresies had so nearly brought him to the gallows.

From Florence Milton went on to Rome, where his scholarly tastes gratified themselves for two months in the study of what remained of the ancient city. The famous picture of Rome in *Paradise Regained* may owe something to these weeks. There, too, he was well received by several of Rome's most distinguished scholars who paid him compliments of Italian extravagance. There, too, he heard the famous Leonora Baroni

sing, and was so moved as to write three
Latin epigrams in her praise. But it was at
Naples, whither he passed on before winter,
that he made the acquaintance which, except
that of Galileo, is the most interesting his
Italian tour brought him. It was that of
the Neopolitan patrician, Giovanni Manso,
who had been intimate with Tasso and
Marini and had been celebrated by Tasso in
the *Gerusalemme Conquistata*. His courtesy
to a foreigner was soon to procure him a still
greater honour; for before leaving Naples
Milton addressed to him a Latin poem thank-
ing him for his kindness, speaking openly of
his own poetic ambitions and praying that, if
he lives to write the great Arthurian Epic
which he was then planning, he may find
such a friend as Tasso found to welcome his
poem, comfort his old age and cherish his
fame. The only difficulty which separated
Manso and Milton was that of religion, where
Milton's unguarded frankness embarrassed
his host. So, when he abandoned his intended tour in Greece because he thought it
" base " to be " travelling abroad at ease for
intellectual culture while his fellow-country-
men were fighting at home for liberty," he
was warned that the Jesuits at Rome had
their eyes on him. But he stayed there two

months nevertheless, fearlessly keeping his resolution, not indeed to introduce or invite religious controversy but, if questioned, then, as he says, " whatsoever I should suffer to dissemble nothing." By February he was again in Florence; and after visits to Bologna, Ferrara and Venice, whence he characteristically shipped " a chest or two of choice music books " for England, he crossed the Alps, spent a week or two at Geneva and in France, and was at home by August 1639.

The elaborate education was now formally complete; and what ordinary men call practical life was at last to begin for Milton. Now for the first time he had an abode of his own, a lodging in St. Bride's, Fleet Street, and soon afterwards a house in Aldersgate Street where he settled with a young nephew whom he undertook to educate. But the real work which he had in view was that of a poet, not of a schoolmaster. The high expectations which he knew he had excited among Italian men of letters had reinforced those of his English friends; and he was now more than ever inclined to follow that " inward prompting which now grew daily upon me that by labour and intent study (which I take to be my portion in this life), joined with the strong propensity of nature, I might perhaps leave something so written to aftertimes as they should not willingly let it die." So, as his extant notes show, he was weighing a large number of subjects for the great poem, slowly settling on a Biblical one, and indeed on that of the Fall of Man, and perhaps writing some earliest lines of what we now know as *Paradise Lost*.

But in November 1640 occurred an event which governed Milton's life for the next twenty years. The Long Parliament met, and, from that time forward till its final meeting in 1660 to dissolve itself and prepare the way for Charles II, politics were the dominant interest of Milton's mind. It is his age of prose; during it he wrote very little verse of any kind, and none of importance except the finer of his eighteen Sonnets which nearly all belong to these years. On the other hand, most of his prose works were written between 1640 and 1660. Of these it is enough to say that they are perhaps the most curious of all illustrations of the great things which a poet alone can bring to prose and of the dangers which he runs in bringing them. A poet of the stature of Milton is ready at all times to catch all kinds of fire, not only the fires of faith and zeal and enthusiasm, but also, as a rule, those of a scorn that knows no limit and a hatred that knows no mercy. Such a man needs a strongly made vessel to control his boiling ardours. Prose is not such a vessel : and they too often overflow from it in extravagance and violence. Poetry in all its severer forms places a restraint upon the poet from which as the mood of art gains upon him he has no desire to escape. Law and limitation, willing obedience to the prescribed conditions, are of the very essence of art. And this is as true of the greatest of the arts as of any other. It is not merely that the poet accepts the bondage of rhymes, or stanzas, or numbered syllables, as the painter accepts those of a flat canvas and the sculptor those of bronze or marble; it is that they all alike submit to the mood of art which is always universal and eternal as well as individual and temporal and therefore disdains such crudities of personal violence as are to be found everywhere in Milton's prose and nowhere in his poetry.

But if a poet's prose has its inevitable disadvantages it has also some great qualities which only a poet can supply. In 1640 Milton plunged into a great struggle in which his attitude throughout was that of an angry and contemptuous partisan. And his pamphlets exhibit all the distortion of facts, in-

justice to opponents, and narrowness of view
which are the inevitable if often unconscious
vices of the man who writes in the interest
of a party. But they also contain flights of
noble eloquence, in which, as in the passage
about the City of London in the *Areopagitica,*
the soul of partisanship has undergone a
fiery purification and emerges free of all its
grosser elements, a pure essence of zeal and
faith and spiritual vision.

The first stage of the struggle was largely
ecclesiastical, and Milton plunged into it with
five pamphlets in 1641 and 1642, fiercely
demanding the abolition of Episcopacy and
the establishment of a Presbyterian system
in England. Fortunately for himself, as he
was soon to see, the views he advocated did
not in the end prevail. For the next step he
took in the way of pamphlet writing would
assuredly have got him into difficulties with
any possible kind of ecclesiastical jurisdiction,
whether after the model of Laud or of Calvin.
It grew out of the most important and disastrous event in the whole of his private life.
In the spring of 1643[1] he went into Oxford-
shire, from which county his father had
originally come, and, to the surprise of his
friends, returned a married man. His wife was

[1] Or 1642, see note p. 6.

Mary Powell, the daughter of a Justice of the
Peace at Forest Hill, near Oxford. The
Powell family owed the Milton family five
hundred pounds, which may have been the
poet's introduction to them. If so, the
marriage to which it led had the results that
might be expected from such a beginning.
The war had then already begun, the King
was at Oxford and the Powells were Cavaliers;
so that when Mrs. Milton, who had been
accompanied to London by her relations, was
to be left alone with a husband of twice her
age, and of severe tastes, she shrank from the
prospect, got away on a visit to her family and
did not return till 1645, by which time the
King was ruined and with him the Powells.

When Shelley deserted his wife he wrote
to her asking her to come and live with him
and the lady who had supplanted her. When
Milton's wife deserted him he wrote a series
of pamphlets advocating divorce at the will
of the husband. Such are the extravagances
of those whose eyes are so accustomed to a
brighter light that when brought into that of
common day they see nothing, and make
mistakes which are justly ridiculous to the
children of this world. It is an old story:
Plato's philosopher in the cave, the saint in
politics, the modern poet in the world of war,

commerce, or industry : the eye that sees
heaven often blunders on earth. Milton's
divorce pamphlets, like nearly all his controversial writings, have three fatal defects.
They are utterly blind to the temper of those
to whom they were addressed, to the reasonable arguments of opponents, and to the
practical difficulties inherent in their proposals. He argues that, as the law gives
relief to a man whose wife disappoints him of
the physical end of marriage, it is an outrage
that he should have none when deprived
of the social and intellectual companionship
which is its moral end. But he takes no note
of the awkward fact that the dismissed wife
is not and cannot be in the same position as
she was before her marriage. Nor does he
give the wife any corresponding rights to get
rid of her husband. These, and a hundred
other difficulties all too visible to duller eyes,
he utterly ignores as he proceeds on his
violent way of deliverance from what he calls
" imaginary and scarecrow sins." Nothing
is allowed to stand in his path. For instance, the awkward texts in the Bible,
whose authority he accepts, are given new
interpretations with which it is to be feared
his temper had more to do than his knowledge of the meaning of Greek words. But

there is not a hint of his own case in all he
says, and it is not desertion that he discusses
but incompatibility of temper. Masson[1] even
sees reason to think that he began the first
pamphlet before his wife left him, but when,
no doubt, her unfitness to be his wife was
only too evident. However all that may be,
we can only think with wondering pity of
those summer weeks of 1643 and of the two
years which followed. Everything in Milton's
life and writings shows him a man unusually
susceptible to the attraction of women, one
whose love was of that strongest sort which is
built on a chastity born not of coldness but of
purity and self-control. Such a man, in such
a plight, with the added misery of knowing
that he owed it to his own rash folly, may be
pardoned for forgetting the true bearing of
his own doctrine that laws are made for the
" common lump of men." Cases like his are
the real tragedies, the tragedies of life so
much more bitter than the more visible ones
of death; and no thinking or feeling man will
lightly decide that they must remain un-
relieved. But neither Milton nor any of his
successors must look at the problem from
his own point of view alone. Laws are
made, and ought to be, as he himself says,
for the " lump of men "; and the wisdom or

[1] See note p. 6.

unwisdom of facilities for divorce must be judged, not merely by the relief they afford in unhappy marriages, but also by the danger of disturbance they produce in the far more numerous marriages which, though experiencing their days of doubt or difficulty, are on the whole happy or at least not unhappy. Perhaps Milton himself might have hesitated if he could have foreseen the consequences of an application of his theories. Modern divorce laws have filled our newspapers with just that "clamouring debate of utterless things" which he dreaded and abhorred, while few will argue that they have increased the number of unions which answer to his conception of "the true intent of marriage."

After all, Milton's own story illustrates the advantages of putting delays and difficulties in the way of divorce. According to his nephew he had planned to act upon his principles and marry " a very handsome and witty gentlewoman "; but the lady had more regard than he to the world's opinion. And she did Milton a service by her reluctance. For the rumour of her, helped by their own misfortunes, brought the Powells to their senses; and with the help of Milton's friends they managed the well-known scene at a room in St. Martin's the Grand, in which he was

surprised by the sight of his wife on her knees
before him.

> " Soon his heart relented
> Towards her, his life so late, and sole delight,
> Now at his feet submissive in distress."

So he glances back at the scene twenty
years later when he was drawing to the close
of his great poem. Meanwhile he received
back his wife, who bore him three daughters
and died in 1653 or 1654. He was to marry
again in 1656; but this second wife, the
" espoused saint " of his sonnet, lived little
more than a year; and in 1663 he married
his third wife who long survived him. But to
return to the house in the Barbican, to which
he removed with his wife in 1645. With him
there were also his father, two nephews and
other boys whom it was his principal occupation to teach. It is somewhat surprising that
he found pupils, as his views on the divorce
question had naturally caused scandal in all
quarters and received little support in any.
He could now see that the Presbyterian
Church discipline which he had advocated so
eagerly in his first pamphlets might have its
inconveniences; the elders of an English
kirk would be no more merciful than his
detested bishops to such freedom of thought,
speech and action as he now demanded.

From henceforth he is an Independent and more than an Independent; for he was attached to no congregation, apparently attended no church regularly, and maintained that profoundly religious temper which is even more visible in his last works than in his first without the support of any authority, creed or companionship in prayer. With these views growing upon him it was natural that, when the struggle came between the Presbyterian Parliament and the Independent Army, he had no hesitation in supporting the Army; nor is it surprising that such a man of no compromise as he had shown himself to be was ready to come forward, even before the deed was done, with a defence of the execution of Charles I. It is in connection with that event that his name first became known to all Europe and was soon so famous that foreigners visiting England desired to see two men above all others, Oliver Cromwell and John Milton. This Milton, from henceforth a European celebrity, was not the author of *Paradise Lost* which was not yet written, nor of his earlier poems which were little known in England and quite unknown elsewhere. He was the apologist of the Regicides, the Foreign Secretary of the world-famed Protector.

For the next eleven years, from 1649 to 1660, Milton had a public and official as well as a private life. Charles was executed on January 30, 1649. Within a few days after appeared Milton's *Tenure of Kings and Magistrates*, largely written, of course, before the execution, and justifying it and all the other proceedings of the Army without any hesitation or compromise. It has some breathings of the Miltonic grandeur; but that is all. For the rest it is a mere party polemic written for the moment; and, as is the case with all pamphlets, the very qualities which gave it its contemporary interest make it unreadable to posterity. Part of it is a sweeping assertion of the inalienable right of the whole people to choose, judge and depose their rulers; a democratic doctrine which a few years later, when England had grown tired of the Army and the Puritans, he was to find as inconvenient as he had already found his early advocacy of the Presbyterian system in matters ecclesiastical. For the moment, however, the pamphlet made him a person of importance. Such a man, learned, eloquent, of high character, of visible sincerity, of utter fearlessness, was not an ally to be despised by a Government which had outraged public opinion at home and abroad. Within a few weeks he was appointed Secretary for Foreign Tongues to the Council of State; and from henceforth till after the death of Cromwell he wrote the weightiest of the vindications, remonstrances and authoritative demands which the great Protector addressed to an astonished and overawed Europe. We can read them still. Many are insignificant, dealing with petty personal details; but the best, especially those that deal with the universal cause of Protestantism and freedom, rise on spiritual wings far above the language of diplomacy and officialism, letting us hear the authentic voice of Milton preluding the thunders of Cromwell and Blake.

But the first important work required of Milton belonged rather to the man of letters than to the Foreign Secretary. The horror aroused both at home and abroad by the execution of Charles, already great enough in itself to be very inconvenient to the Government, was greatly increased by the publication of a book called *Eikon Basilike* which purported to be the work of the king himself and appeared immediately after his death. It is a kind of religious portrait of Charles, reporting his spiritual meditations and containing a justification of his life. Its success was prodigious; fifty editions are said

to have appeared within a year. It was
obviously necessary that some reply should
be attempted; and the task was naturally
assigned to Milton, who published his *Eikonoklastes*, or Image-Breaker, in October. It is a
mere pamphlet, even more violent than the
Tenure of Kings, not ashamed to rake up such
absurdities as the alleged poisoning of James I
by Buckingham, with the usual Miltonic
inconsistencies, such as that which denounces
Charles for the crime of refusing his consent
to bills passed by Parliament and forgets
that the Government on whose behalf he is
writing established itself by a forcible sup-
pression of the Parliamentary majority. It
survives now only by the curious passage in it
which tells us that William Shakspeare was
" the closet companion " of Charles I in the
" solitudes " of the end of his life; and by
the puritanical allusion to the " vain amatori-
ous poem of Sir Philip Sidney's *Arcadia* "
from which, however " full of worth and wit "
in its own kind, it was a disgrace to the king
to borrow a prayer at so grave an hour.
Perhaps as a mark of their approval of *Eikonoklastes*, the Council of State gave Milton lodg-
ings in Whitehall; and soon afterwards, in
January 1650, called upon him to reply to
another Royalist book which was making a

great stir. The result was the beginning of a political and personal controversy which lasted almost as long as it was safe for Milton to write about politics at all.

In the sixteenth and seventeenth centuries great scholars had a position which they are never likely to occupy again. In those cosmopolitan days when an Italian governed France, and regiments and even armies were often commanded by foreigners, the honour of possessing a celebrated scholar was eagerly disputed not only by universities, but by cities, sovereign states, and even kings. Learning had then a market value in the world : for then, as always, especially since the invention of printing, European opinion was worth having on one's side; and in the days before journalism the practice was to hire distinguished scholars to write to a political brief. After the death of Charles I it was obviously the policy of Charles II to secure support by a powerful indictment of the iniquity of the rulers of the English Commonwealth. For this purpose his advisers obtained the services of a certain Claude de Saumaise, or, as he was generally called, Salmasius. This man, forgotten now except for Milton, was then a scholar of such fame that his presence was disputed between Oxford and Venice, the French and the Dutch, between the Pope who wanted him at Rome and Christina of Sweden who was soon to persuade him to go to Stockholm. So it is not altogether surprising that Charles II was advised to pay him, and perhaps paid him, much more than he could afford for writing a book called *Defensio Regia*, which was to be before all Europe the public statement of the case against the new rulers of England. Milton spent a year in preparing his reply, which came out in the beginning of 1651. The *Pro Populo Anglicano Defensio* is now pleasanter reading for Milton's detractors than for those who honour his name. The unbridled insults which it heaps upon Charles I and still more upon Salmasius, for whom its least offensive titles are such as " blockhead," " liar " and " apostate," exceed even the wide limits of abuse customary in these days. *Corruptio optimi pessima :* such a man as Milton, if he once descends to the bandying of foul language, will beat the very bargemen themselves. But what astonished his contemporaries was not his violence but his courage. An unknown Englishman had dared to meet the giant of learning on his own ground and had at least held his own. It may have been partly as the result of this

that Salmasius no longer found Holland a
pleasant place of residence and removed to
Sweden. A more certain result is that the
English David who had stood up to Goliath
was from henceforth a European celebrity.
With his usual proud courage he had put his
own name on the title-page of his book,
challenging to himself both the glories and
the dangers that might come of it. He was
not to be disappointed of either.

From henceforth he was in the thick of a
violent controversy, which made so much
more noise than it deserved in its own day
that it need make none here. Replies came
out both to his *Eikonoklastes* and to his
Defensio : new books grew out of the controversy; Milton's nephew wrote on his behalf, and anonymous friends of Salmasius on
his; the adversaries of Milton no more spared
his character than he had spared theirs; a
Defensio Secunda from his own hand seemed
necessary, and appeared in 1654; and so with
minor pamphlets and second editions we get
on to the end of the weary controversy, in
which for contemporaries there was perhaps
some fire and light, but for us now little but
smoke and darkness of confusion.

Such was the work which was Milton's chief
occupation during the Commonwealth, to the

doing of which he deliberately sacrificed his
eyesight. Within a year after the publication of his book against Salmasius its foreseen
result was complete. From henceforth Milton
was dependent upon the eyes of others. He
was only forty-four when overtaken by this
calamity. Yet his courage seems never to
have failed him. " I argue not," he tells
Cyriack Skinner in his sonnet—

> " Against Heaven's hand or will, nor bate a
>   jot
>   Of heart or hope, but still bear up and
>   steer
> Right onward. What supports me, dost
>   thou ask ?
>   The conscience, friend, to have lost them
>   overplied
>   In Liberty's defence, my noble task,
> Of which all Europe rings from side to side."

Whoever had begun to have doubts about
the course taken in 1649 and since, he had
none ; and no one had suffered more in defence
of it. The other and greater sonnet on his
blindness—

> " When I consider how my light is spent
>   Ere half my days in this dark world and
>   wide "

shows him content if need be to take his
place among those whose desire to serve

God must find its peace in the thought that

"They also serve who only stand and wait."

In the same spirit are the words, characteristically altered from those of St. Paul, which he wrote in an album in 1651: "I am made perfect in weakness." But nothing of weakness, not even its perfection, could ever come near Milton. He played a greater part in this world without his eyes than ever he had played with them. Without their help he did what prose could do towards justifying the ways of England to Europe, and was very soon to do what verse could do towards justifying the ways of God to men. He cannot, perhaps, be said to have succeeded in either, but one at least of the failures is a whole heaven above what ordinary men call success.

A few words may be said of his attitude towards men and measures during this political period of his life. His unqualified and immediate support of the King's execution had, of course, united him with the Cromwellian party who had brought it about. And his anti-Presbyterian views carried him in the same direction. So we are not surprised to find that, when Cromwell got rid of the Parliament by military force and soon after-

wards became Protector, Milton approved his
action and gladly continued to serve under
him. Nor was Milton the man to be disturbed by the Protector's rapid dissolution
of his first Parliament, by the period of
personal Government which followed, or by
his angry breach with his second Parliament.
Poets have seldom understood politics, and
Milton, the most political of poets, perhaps
less than any. No man ever had less of that
sense of law and custom, of the need of continuity, which is the very centre and secret
of politics. Few great statesmen have been
able to maintain perfect consistency; but the
least consistent have generally been aware
that there was something in inconsistencies
that needed explanation. Milton never shows
any consciousness of the patent incongruity
between his early exaltation of the indefeasible
rights of Parliaments and his support of the
Cromwellian attitude towards them : between
his angry denunciation of Charles I for pre-
suming to retain the ancient right of the
kings to refuse their assent to Bills submitted
to them and his approval of Cromwell's dis-
missal of a Parliament for attempting to deny
the same right to the Protector : between the
extreme doctrine of free printing claimed in
the *Areopagitica* and the fact that its author

was afterwards concerned in licensing books under a Government which vigorously suppressed " seditious " publications. But inconsistencies by themselves are of little importance, particularly in revolutionary times; they would be of none, in Milton's case, if he had ever admitted that he had learnt from experience and consequently changed his mind. But he never did. Parliaments remained sacred when they were for pulling down bishops, profane when they were for establishing Presbyterianism, and utterly detestable when they were for restoring Charles II. The fact is, of course, that Milton, like most men of much imagination and no political experience, saw a vision of certain things in the value of which he believed with all his soul, and saw none of the objections to them and none of the difficulties that stood in their way. At the very end, when the bonfires for Charles II were almost lighted in the streets, he could publish *A Ready and Easy Way to Establish a Free Commonwealth ;* and the title he chose for that book was typical of his whole attitude in all practical matters. He had to an extreme degree the man of vision's blindness to the all-important fact that the mass of men would not have what he aims at if they

c

could and could not if they would. At least
in a free country the statesman knows that
he has got to work through stupid people,
with their consent, and with regard to the
measure of their capacities. For such men
as Milton stupid people either do not exist or
are to be merely ignored. That is his attitude
all through. Alike in the matter of divorce
and in the matter of education, in the ecclesiastical problem and in the political, he was
always eager to put forward a "ready and
easy way" which entirely ignored the nature
of the human material which was to walk in it.
He simply chose not to see that in all these
matters men had for centuries been walking
in a way which was not his, a way which
had in fact by now diverged many miles
from his; and that they could not possibly,
even if they would, transport themselves in a
moment, at a mere wave of his wand, across
the intervening bogs and forests which the
lapse of years had rendered impassable. He
never appears to have had a single glimpse
of the truth that the essential business of
the statesman is to be always moving from
the past to the future without ever letting the
bridge between them break down. The principal food of a political people is custom, and to
break the bridge is to cut off the only source

of its supply. The greatest proof that Cromwell was really a statesman and not a mere political emergency man of unusual character and ability is that in his last years he was evidently seeing more and more plainly that the right metaphor for a statesman is taken from grafting and not from " root and branch " operations. It is clear that he had seen that political branches may be pruned away but roots can very seldom be safely disturbed; and that among the roots in English politics were a hereditary Monarchy and an established Church. Dynasty and formularies might perhaps be safely changed; but the things themselves were of the root, and the tree would not flourish if they were touched. It is characteristic of Milton that in both these matters he was strongly opposed to the policy towards which Cromwell was feeling his way. Ten years had taught him nothing, and the death of Cromwell found him as blind to political possibilities as the death of Charles I.

One would like to know something of the relations between the two greatest men of the Commonwealth. But there is little or nothing to know. It is plain that in most matters they must have been in close agreement; and in a few, as in the business of the

Piedmont massacres, the two great hearts
must have beaten as one, while the sword
of Cromwell stood ready drawn behind the
trumpet of Milton's noble prose and nobler
verse. The only surviving act of personal
contact between them is to be found in
Milton's sonnet; and that is a public tribute
with no suggestion of private intimacy in it.
Indeed, as Masson has pointed out, it may
easily be taken to mean more than it really
does; for it was not written because Milton
could not keep silence about his admiration
of Cromwell, but rather, as its full title shows,
as a petition or appeal to Cromwell to save
the nation from parliamentary proposals for
the setting up of a State Church and for
limiting the toleration of dissent from it.
The sonnet, then, proves less than it has
sometimes been made to prove; and in any
case it proves no intimacy. Perhaps after
all, in the case of Milton as in that of most
men who deal with public affairs, we are apt
to exaggerate the importance in their daily
lives of these visible official activities. The
world thinks it knows men who fight battles,
or make speeches, or write books; but it
knows nothing of their private thoughts or
studies and still less of their private loves
and joys and sorrows which to themselves

and in truth are much the most real part
of their lives. So with Milton during these
years; his wife and little children may have
been, his second wife and such friends as
Cyriack Skinner and Henry Lawrence and
Lady Ranelagh and the poet Marvell certainly
were, much greater realities to him in his
daily thoughts than either the hated Salmasius
and Morus of the pamphlets or the admired
Cromwell of the sonnet. The "weekly table"
he is said to have kept, at the expense of the
State, for foreign ministers, must have provided interesting talk; but the true Milton
cannot have lived in these gatherings so fully
at the time or remembered them afterwards
so affectionately as those other more intimate
parties of which he gives us a picture in the
two sonnets to Lawrence and Skinner which,
for lovers of poetry, look so pleasantly back
to Horace and so pleasantly forward to
Cowper and Tennyson.

" Lawrence, of virtuous father virtuous son,
    Now that the fields are dank, and ways
      are mire,
    Where shall we sometimes meet, and by
      the fire
    Help waste a sullen day, what may be
      won
From the hard season gaining? Time will
    run

On smoother, till Favonius re-inspire
The frozen earth, and clothe in fresh
    attire
The lily and rose, that neither sowed nor
    spun.
What neat repast shall feast us, light and
    choice,
Of Attic taste, with wine, whence we may
    rise
To hear the lute well touched, or artful
    voice
Warble immortal notes and Tuscan air?
He who of those delights can judge, and
    spare
To interpose them oft, is not unwise."

This is his own graver and older parallel to
what his nephew tells us of his schoolmastering
days when he would turn from " hard study
and spare diet " to " drop once a month or
so into the society of some young sparks of
his acquaintance," and with them " would so
far make bold with his body as now and then
to keep a gawdy day." The sonnet shows
that the poet is still the poet of *L'Allegro* and
Il Penseroso, no narrow fanatic, but a lover
of company and the arts, and of the richness
and fulness of life. Such occasions as that
it describes must have been oases in the
desert of controversy and public business
abroad and of blindness and loneliness at
home. He did not live long in Whitehall,

moving in 1652 to a house overlooking St.
James's Park, near what is now Queen Anne's
Gate. There his first wife died in 1653, or
1654, and her short-lived successor too; there
he lived during the remaining years of the
Commonwealth, working at his pamphlets and
State papers, even beginning *Paradise Lost*,
with young friends to read to him, write for
him, lead their blind great man about in the
Park or elsewhere, till the catastrophe of 1660
arrived and it was no longer safe for the
defender of Regicide to be seen in the streets.

Why Milton was not hanged at the Restoration is still something of a mystery. His
name must have been more hatefully known
to the returning exiles than that of any one
except the dead Cromwell whose death did
not save his body from a grim ceremony at
Tyburn. He had not only defended Charles
I's execution before all Europe, and in a tone
almost of exultation, but he had pursued the
whole Stuart family with vituperation and
contempt. Even in the very last weeks, when
the bells were already almost ringing for
Charles II, he had dared to raise his voice
against the " abjured and detested thraldom
of kingship "; declaring that he would not be
silent though he should but speak " to trees
and stones : and had none to cry to, but

with the prophet ' O Earth, Earth, Earth ! '
to tell the very soil itself what her perverse
inhabitants are deaf to,"—a passage, if inter-
preted by its original context, of awful im-
precation upon Charles II   A man so famous,
so utterly unrepentant, so defiant to the very
end, seemed to challenge to himself the gallows.
That his challenge would receive its natural
answer was the openly expressed opinion of his
enemies.   No doubt it was also the fear of his
friends, who concealed him in Smithfield from
May till August 1660.   By the 24th of August
the danger was over.   The Act of Indemnity,
which was a pardon to all political offenders
not by name excepted in it, became law on
that day; and Milton's was not one of the
excepted names.   How was that managed ?
There are various stories; perhaps each has
some truth in it; many influences may have
combined.   One is that he had saved Davenant
in his danger some years before and now the
Cavalier poet in his turn saved the Puritan.
But Davenant was not in Parliament, and the
real work must have been done by a group of
friends who were.   The most important of
them seem to have been Annesley (afterwards
Lord Anglesey), Sir Thomas Clarges, who
was Monk's brother-in-law, Monk's secretary
Morrice, and the poet's less powerful but

still more devoted friend Andrew Marvell.
Between them somehow they saved him,
aided no doubt by the general pity for a
blind man, the general respect for his learning which found expression even in that
moment and even in Royalist pamphlets,
and, one may hope, by the knowledge of a
few of them that this was a man of genius
from whom there might be great things yet
to come.   The names of those who thus made
possible the greatest poem in the English
language deserve lasting record; and a word
of gratitude may be added to Clarendon and
to Charles II for refraining from saying the
easy and not unnatural word which would
have been instantly fatal to their old enemy.

The odd thing is that he was arrested after
all.   There had been an order of the House
of Commons for his arrest and for the burning
of his books, possibly, as Masson thinks,
obtained by his friends to make it seem
unnecessary to except him in the Indemnity
Bill.   The books were duly burnt, or such
copies of them as came to the hands of the
hangman; and ultimately, at some uncertain
date, Milton himself was got into the custody
of the Sergeant-at-Arms.   He was soon re-
leased, and the story would not be worth
relating but for a curious proof it gives of the
c 2

obstinate courage of the poet. The House
ordered his release on December 15; and one
would have supposed that he would have
been glad to escape into obscurity and safety
again on any terms. But no; the Sergeant-
at-Arms demanded high fees which Milton
thought unreasonable; and even then, when
he had almost felt the hangman's rope on
his neck, he would not be bullied by any
man. He refused to pay: and though the
Solicitor-General ominously remarked that he
deserved hanging, his friends got the fees
referred to a committee and presumably
reduced. Before the beginning of 1661 he
was definitely a free man to live his final
fourteen years of political defeat, isolation
and silence, of unparalleled poetic fertility, and,
before the end, of acknowledged poetic fame.

He did not return any more to the fashionable and therefore dangerous neighbourhood
of Whitehall, but lived the rest of his life in a
succession of houses in or near the city, ending
in Artillery Walk, Bunhill Fields, where he
died. His friends must for years have feared
that he might be attacked and perhaps
murdered by some drunken Cavalier revellers
accidentally coming across the old regicide.
And in spite of the Act of Indemnity he can
hardly have felt absolutely comfortable on

the side of the law when so late as 1664 his *Tenure of Kings* was denounced by the censor as still extant and an unfortunate printer was hanged, drawn and quartered for issuing a sort of new version of it. Misfortunes without and fears within might be the summing up, if not of the poet's, at least of the man's life during these first years after the Restoration. To begin with, he was a much poorer man. His salary as Secretary was, of course, gone. But besides that he had lost £2000, equal to about £7000 now, which he had invested in Commonwealth Securities, as well as some confiscated property he had bought of the Chapter of Westminster; and he was soon to lose, at least temporarily, the rent he received from his father's house in Bread Street which was destroyed by the Fire of London. Masson calculates that he was left after the Restoration with an income about equal to £700 of our money which his further losses and outlay on his daughters had reduced to £300 or £350 before his death; not quite poverty even at the end, but something very different from what the eldest son of a rich man had been accustomed to. A graver misfortune was the gout which afflicted him for the rest of his life and gave him so much pain that he made little of his blindness in comparison with it. Worst of all was his unhappy relation to his daughters. That is the ugliest thing in the story of his life. How things might have gone with his son, if the baby boy had lived, one does not know; but his oriental views of the moral and intellectual inferiority of women, which doubled the dangers of their fascinations, made him certain to be a despotic father to three motherless girls. And so he was. He had plenty of young men eager for the privilege of reading to him : but of course they could not be always with him, and the result was that dreadful picture which comes to us from his nephew, no unfriendly witness, of the daughters " condemned to the performance of reading and exactly pronouncing of all the languages of whatever book he should at one time or other think fit to peruse; viz. the Hebrew (and, I think, the Syriac), the Greek, the Latin, the Italian, Spanish and French," none of which languages they understood. Nor did he show any desire that they should; saying grimly that one tongue was enough for a woman. History and fiction are alike full of the tragedies that result from the blindness of extraordinary minds to ordinary duties; and Milton's case is one of the saddest. The daughters cheated him and made away with

his books; he spoke of them gravely and
repeatedly as his " unkind children "; one of
them is even reported, on very good evidence,
to have said, at his third marriage in 1663,
that " that was no news to hear of his wedding
but, if she could hear of his death, that was
something." At last it was thought better
that he and they should part; and they were
put out, at considerable expense to their
father, to learn embroidery work and other
" curious and ingenious manufactures " for
their living. It is pleasant to hear that the
youngest, Deborah, who was visited by
Addison not long before he died, and received
fifty guineas from Queen Caroline, was " in a
transport " of delight when shown a portrait
of her father, crying out " 'Tis my father, 'tis
my dear father, I see him; 'tis him; 'tis the
very man ! here, here ! " as she pointed to
some of the features. So one likes to be told,
on her authority, that he was delightful company and " the life of the conversation, full
of unaffected cheerfulness and civility " when
he had his l'ttle parties of friends. And to
us, if not to her, it is a pleasant story that she
could still repeat many lines from Homer,
Euripides and Ovid, though she said she did
not understand Greek or Latin. The wife of
a Spitalfields weaver must at last have felt

some pride in these survivals of her childish drudgery, proof audible to all men, if to her unintelligible, that she was the daughter of Mr. Milton, the great scholar and poet.

No more need to be said of sorrow or failure. The rest is a serene and productive old age. *Paradise Lost* was published in 1667, *Paradise Regained* and *Samson* in 1671. Besides these there was, in 1673, a new edition of his earlier poems reprinted, with additions from that of 1645; and many publications of prose works mostly written in earlier years but never printed, such as his *History of Britain*, and little books on Education, Logic and Grammar. He kept up his strenuous life of study and composition apparently to the end. He is said to have got up at four or five in the morning, and, after hearing a chapter or two from the Hebrew Bible and breakfasting, to have passed the five hours before his midday dinner dictating or having some book read to him. In the afternoon he would walk a little in his garden; all his life a garden had been one of the things he would not do without. Then music and more private study carried him on to an Horatian supper of olives or other " light things "; and so to a pipe of tobacco, a glass of water and bed. He drank but little wine, and that only with his meals.

Such a way of life deserved a healthful old age, which, but for that healthy man's disease the gout, he had, and a death such as he had, so easy as to be imperceptible to the bystanders. That was on November 8, 1674. Four days later his body was buried in the church of St. Giles, Cripplegate, where his grave may still be seen; the funeral being accompanied by " all his learned and great friends in London, not without a concourse of the vulgar."

By that time the battle of his life had been won. The astonishing achievements of his last years had more than fulfilled the high promise and proud words of his long distant youth. Perhaps no seven years in all literary history provide a finer record of poetic genius triumphing over difficulties external and internal than these last seven of Milton's life from 1667 to 1674. They had their reward and not only from posterity. There is a still lingering delusion, based chiefly on the five pounds paid for the first edition of *Paradise Lost*, that Milton's greatness was little recognized in his lifetime. The truth is the exact reverse. He had far more chance of hearing his own praises, if he cared for that, than most of the great English poets : than Keats and Shelley, for instance; than Wordsworth,

at least till he was old; nay, in all probability
than Shakspeare himself. Which of them
heard the most popular poet of their day say
of them anything at all like Dryden's famous
and generous " This man cuts us all out and
the ancients too "? It is not even true that
Paradise Lost sold badly. On the contrary,
in a year and a half from the day of publication over thirteen hundred copies had been
sold, from which the author received £10
and the publisher, it is believed, £50 or £60.
He would be a sanguine publisher to-day who
would be quite certain of making in eighteen
months the modern equivalent of this sum,
say £180, out of a new epic, even if it were
as great as Milton's.

But the money question was not of the first
importance to Milton and is of none to us.
The interesting thing is the almost immediate
recognition of the greatness of the poem.
Nothing in the world could be more alien to
the tone of the society and literature of the
London of Charles II than this long Biblical
Puritan poem with its scarcely veiled attacks
on the revived Monarchy and Episcopacy and
its entirely unveiled attacks on the fashionable
men of Belial. Yet it was from the very high
priests of this society that the most unstinted
praise came. Of its professional men of

letters Dryden was already rapidly advancing
to the unquestioned primacy which was soon
to be his, and to remain his for his life; of its
amateurs Lord Dorset had perhaps the most
brilliant reputation. It was these two men
who, more than any others, made the town
recognize the greatness of Milton. Both were
as unlike Milton as men could be, and Dryden
had just committed himself to a strong
championship of rhymed verse as against
blank. There is nowhere a finer proof of the
compelling power of great art upon those who
know it when they see it than the unbounded
praise with which Dryden at once saluted
Milton. The fact that his admiration at first
took the absurd form of turning Milton's epic
into a " heroic opera " in rhyme does not
detract from the significance of his writing
publicly within a year of Milton's death that
the blind old regicide's poem was " one of
the greatest, most noble and sublime which
either this age or nation has produced," and
to this he was to add, thirteen years later, the
still bolder tribute of the well-known epigram
about " three poets in three distant ages born "
which gives Milton a place above Homer and
Virgil. The lines are in detail absurd; but
their absurdity does not destroy the fact that
the intellectual life of England was never

keener, or more eager to welcome talent in
art or letters, than in the reign of Charles II;
and nothing is clearer proof of it than the
honours received by the rebel Milton from a
Court composer like Henry Lawes, a Court
physician like Samuel Barrow, a statesman
and minister like Lord Anglesey, and a poet
laureate like Dryden.

So we may think of him happily enough
in these last years. He had now done the
work which from his early manhood he had
felt it was his task in life to do. When he
was not much over thirty he had boldly
written in public of what his mind, "in the
spacious circuits of her musing, hath liberty
to propose to herself, though of highest hope
and hardest attempting; whether that epic
form whereof the two poems of Homer, and
those other two of Virgil and Tasso, are a
diffuse and the book of Job a brief model . . .
or whether those dramatic constitutions,
wherein Sophocles and Euripides reign, shall
be found more doctrinal and exemplary to a
nation." For the moment nothing seemed
to come of these high words; but before he
died not one only, but both of his dreams,
the drama as well as the epic, were accomplished facts. *Paradise Lost,* begun as a
drama, had become the greatest of modern

epics; and the abandoned drama had reappeared in *Samson*, not the greatest of English tragedies, but the one which best recalls the peculiar greatness of the drama of Greece. Self-confident young men have always been common enough, but there are two differences between them and Milton : their performance falls far short of their promise instead of exceeding it; and neither promise nor performance is marked by this exalting and purifying sense of a thing divinely inspired and divinely aided. Such work can wait, as his did, being such as is "not to be raised from the heat of youth or the vapours of wine; like that which flows at waste from the pen of some vulgar amourist, or the trencher fury of a rhyming parasite; nor to be obtained by the invocation of dame memory and her siren daughters, but by devout prayer to that eternal Spirit who can enrich with all utterance and knowledge, and sends out his seraphim, with the hallowed fire of his altar, to touch and purify the lips of whom he pleases."

Now the task is done; and he can sit alone in his upstairs room in Artillery Walk and thank God that in spite of blindness, private sorrows and public disappointments, he had been enabled at last to bear the witness of a work of immortal beauty to the high truth that had been in him even from a boy. So it may have been in the graver moments of solitude; while, as we know from several sources, there were other times, when he would enjoy the companionship of friends and the homage of learned strangers by whom we are told he was "much visited, more than he did desire." The picture suggested to us is that of a man who at sixty-five, then a greater age than now, retained all his powers of mind and much of the physical beauty which had been so remarkable in his youth; who was gracious but somewhat reserved and dignified with strangers; a delightful companion to friends and especially to younger men; full of literature, especially of poetry, and with a memory that enabled him to recite long passages from Homer and Virgil; above all, an ardent lover of music, making a practice, so far as possible, of hearing some, whether vocal or instrumental, every afternoon. His ears were eyes to him; and when he heard a lady sing finely he would say: "Now will I swear this lady is handsome." All kinds of music, and not only the severer, were delightful to the "organ-voice of England."

That is not the least interesting thing about him. The greatest of England's Puritans was also the greatest of her artists. He had nothing in him of the morbid scrupulosity which is such an inhuman feature in French Jansenism and some of the English sects. His was a large nature which demanded a free expansion of life. Lonely figure as he is in our literary history, with no real predecessors or followers, his mighty arch yet bridges the gulf between Elizabeth and the Revolution, and is of nearer or less distant kin to Shakspeare than to Pope. His prose is the swan song of the old eloquence, as inspired and as confused as an oracle. To read it when it is at its best is to soar on wings through the empyrean and despise Swift and Addison walking in neat politeness on the pavement. There as everywhere, in his verse, in his character, in his mind, in his life, he has the strength and the weakness of an aristocrat. The youth who in his Cambridge days was " esteemed a virtuous person yet not to be ignorant of his parts " did not belie the opinion formed of him in either of those respects. His Republicanism was of the proud Roman sort, and at least as near Coriolanus as Gracchus; a boundless faith in the State and a boundless desire to spend and be spent in its service, a total and scornful indifference to the opinions of all

those, though they might be five-sixths of
the nation, who did not desire to be served in
the way which he had decided to be for their
good. The modern way of deciding matters
of State by counting heads may very likely
be the best of many unsatisfactory ways of
accomplishing a very difficult business; but
it has always been peculiarly exasperating to
men of genius who see their way plainly and
cannot understand why a million blind men
are to keep them out of it. Milton liked the
voice of the majority well enough when he
could plead it against Charles I; but when
he found it calling for Charles II he treated
it as a mere impertinent absurdity; the vain
babble of a " misguided and abused multi-
tude " with whom wise men have nothing to
do except to keep them in their place. And
it is in the latter attitude that he is most
really himself. His is, of course, an aris-
tocracy of mind and character, not of birth
and wealth; but the self-sufficient scorn
which was almost a virtue in Aristotle's eyes,
and is in ours the besetting sin of even the
noblest of aristocrats, is too frequent a note
in all his prose, and even in his poetry; and
it is sometimes poured out upon those who
are fitter subjects for tenderness than for
contempt. One can scarcely imagine a child

or an ignorant man being quite at ease in
Milton's company.

But these are the penalties that greatness
has too often to pay for being itself. So long
as we remain human beings and not divine,
it will be found hard to unite humility, ease
of manner, and the glad sufferance of fools
with a mind struggling in a storm of sublime
thoughts, with powers that are and know
themselves to be far above those of ordinary
men. It will never be easy for men of supreme
genius to behave to their inferiors as if they
were their equals. But that is not the side
of Milton of which we ought to think most
often now. It is more just as well as more
merciful to him, and it is of more use to
ourselves, to fix our eyes on his strength,
and not on the weakness that more or less
inevitably accompanied it. The ancients admired strength more than the moderns have,
at least until lately. But no one can refuse
to admire such strength as Milton's, so continuous, so triumphant over exceptional ob-
stacles, so disdainful of all petty or personal
ends. There is a majesty about it to which
one scarcely knows any real parallel. Strength
implies purpose and art implies unity of conception; the instinct of art was only less strong
in Milton than the resolute will; so that it

is not surprising that scarcely any life has such unity as his. It is itself a perfect work of art. If we put aside, as we may fairly, the partial political inconsistencies, the rest is absolutely of one piece; a great building, nobly planned from the beginning and nobly executed to the last harmonious detail of the original design. We men are, most of us, weak creatures who accomplish but the tiniest fragments of even such poor designs as we make for our lives. There is something that uplifts us in the spectacle of the triumphant completion of so great a plan as the life of Milton. We are exalted by the thought that, after all, we are of the same flesh and blood, nay, even of the same breed, as this wonderful man. To read the *Paradise Lost* is to realize, in the highest degree, how the poet's imagination can impose a majestic order on the tumultuous confusion of human speech and knowledge. To read its author's life is to realize, with equally exalting clearness, how a strong man's will can so victoriously mould a world of adverse circumstances that affliction, defeat—nay, even the threatening shadow of death itself—are made the very instruments by which he becomes that which he has, from the beginning of his years, chosen for himself to be.

CHAPTER III

THE EARLIER POEMS

WE think to-day of Milton chiefly as the author of *Paradise Lost*, as we think of Wren as the builder of St. Paul's. And we are right. When a man has been the creator of the only very great building in the world which bears upon it from the first stone to the last the mark of a single mind, his other achievements, even though they include Greenwich, Hampton Court, Trinity College Library, and some fifty churches, inevitably fall into the background. So when the world has admitted that a poet has disputed the supreme palm of epic with Homer and Virgil, it hardly cares to remember that he has also challenged all rivals in such forms as the Pastoral Elegy, the Mask, and the Sonnet. *De minimis non curat* might be applied to such cases without any very violent extravagance. The first thought that must always rise to the mind at the mention of Milton's name must be the stupendous achievement of *Paradise Lost*.

Yet if Milton had been hanged at Tyburn

in 1660 he would still unquestionably rank
with the half-dozen greatest of the English
poets. Chaucer and Spenser would then have
ranked after Shakspeare as higher names
than his : and possibly also Wordsworth,
Keats and Shelley. But he could have feared
no other rival : for Dryden is too much a
mere man of letters, Pope too much a mere
wit, Byron too exclusively a rhetorician,
Tennyson too exclusively an artist, to rank
with a man in whom burned the divine fire
of *Lycidas* and the great Ode. What would
Milton's fame have rested upon if he had
not lived to write *Paradise Lost* and its two
successors ? Upon the volume published in
the year 1645, the year of Naseby, when
people, one would have supposed, were not
thinking much of poetry, and those who were
most likely to be doing so were just those
least inclined to look for it from John Milton,
the Puritan pamphleteer. Yet in that little
book was heard for the last time the voice,
now raised above itself, of the old poetry
which the Cavaliers and courtiers had loved.

No single volume has ever contained so
much fine English verse by an unknown
or almost unknown poet. It is true that
Lycidas and *Comus* had been printed before,
but *Comus* had appeared anonymously and

Lycidas had been signed only with initials.
So that only friends, or people behind the
scenes in the literary world, could know anything of Milton's poetry.   Nor does he seem
to have been very anxious that they should.
The other contributors to the volume in
memory of Edward King gave their names:
the only signature to *Lycidas* is **J. M.**   It was
Lawes the composer, not Milton the author,
who published *Comus* in 1637.   Milton's
feelings about it are indicated by the motto
on the title page—

" Eheu quid volui misero mihi I floribus
　　Austrum
　　Perditus—"

Quotations can often say for us what we
cannot say for ourselves.   What Virgil says
for Milton is " Alas what is this that I have
done? poor fool that I am, could not I have
kept my tender buds of verse a little longer
from the cutting blasts of public criticism? "
Yet no one knew better than Milton that
Comus was incomparably the greatest of the
masks.   So in the sonnet on reaching the
age of twenty-three he says that his " late
spring no bud or blossom shew'th."   Yet he
had already written the *Ode on the Nativity*,
a performance sufficient, one would have

thought, to give a young poet reasonable
self-satisfaction in what he had done, as well
as confidence in what he would be able to do.
Nor was Milton in the ordinary sense, or perhaps in any, a humble man. Of that false
kind of humility, too often recommended
from the pulpit, which consists in a beautiful
woman trying to suppose herself plain, or an
able man trying to be unaware of his ability,
no man ever had less than Milton. Neither
from himself nor from others did he ever con-
ceal the fact that he was a man of genius.
In his eyes no kind of untruth, however
specious, could be a virtue. But of a finer
humility, built on truth, he was not without
his share. The truly humble man may be a
genius and may know it and may never affect
to deny it : he may know that he has done
great things, far greater than have been done
by the men he sees around him : but he is
not judging himself by the standard of other
men : he has another standard, that of " the
perfect witness of all-judging Jove," that of
" as ever in my great Taskmaster's eye," and
of that he knows how very far he has fallen
short. Of this nobler humility Milton had
something all his life and in his youth much.
It is this which reconciles the apparent inconsistency between his many proud con-

fessions that he knows himself to be a man
called to do great things and his reluctance
to let the world see what he had already done :
between his keeping *L'Allegro* and *Il Penseroso* ten years unpublished and his preserving
and ultimately publishing almost everything
he had ever written, even to scraps of boyish
and undergraduate verse. From one point of
view his best was nothing : from the other,
more than equally true, the humblest line
that had come from his pen had received a
passport to immortality.

What does the famous volume contain?
It opens with the noble *Ode on the Nativity*,
as if to give the discerning reader invincible
proof in the first twenty lines put before him
that the proud words of the publisher's preface
were amply justified. " Let the event guide
itself which way it will, I shall deserve of the
age by bringing into the light as true a birth
as the Muses have brought forth since our
famous Spenser wrote ; whose poems in these
English ones are as rarely imitated as sweetly
excelled. Reader, if thou art eagle-eyed to
censure their worth, I am not fearful to expose
them to thy exactest perusal." So the preface
ends : and then what follows is—

" This is the month, and this the happy morn,
  Wherein the Son of Heaven's Eternal King,

Of wedded maid and virgin mother born,
Our great redemption from above did bring;
For so the holy sages once did sing,
    That he our deadly forfeit should release,
And with his Father work us a perpetual
    peace."

Magnus ab integro saeclorum nascitur ordo.
No one had ever written such English verse
as this before : no one ever would again.
Here was a poet, writing at the age of twenty-
one, for whom it was evident that no theme
could be so high that he could not find it fit
utterance. Fit and also peculiar to himself.
The peculiar Miltonic note which none of his
innumerable imitators have ever caught for
more than a few lines, which he himself never
in all his works loses for more than a moment,
is instantly struck. As Mr. Mackail has said,
" there is not a square inch of his poetry from
first to last of which one could not confidently
say, ' This is Milton and no one else.' " One
may even go further than Mr. Mackail. For
he seems to make an exception where certainly none is needed. He is justly insisting
that one of the most remarkable things about
Milton is that, while English poetry spoke
one language in his youth and another in his
age, he himself spoke neither. His " accent
and speech " alike in *Lycidas* and in *Paradise*

Lost are his own, and in marked contrast to
those of contemporary poets. But here Mr.
Mackail adds the qualification " if we exclude
a few slight juvenile pieces of his boyhood
and those metrical versions of the Psalms in
which he elected not to be a poet." He
asserts, that is, that neither in the Psalms
nor in the " juvenile pieces " is Milton
characteristically himself and that in the
Psalms he is not a poet at all. And no one
will care to deny that many of the versions
of the Psalms have little Milton and less
poetry in them. But is this true of all?
And in particular is it true of the paraphrase
of Psalm CXXXVI. which, with its companion
version of Psalm CXIV. is the most "juvenile"
of all? A boy of fifteen has not usually
much power of " electing " to be or not to be
a poet. But it can only be inadvertence on
Mr. Mackail's part that would deny that the
boy Milton at that age, though not a great
poet, was already himself and, more than
that, was already promising what he was
soon to perform. Who, looking back from
the *Ode* and *Comus* and *Paradise Lost*, does
not hear some preluding of the authentic
strain of Milton in

" Who by his all-commanding might
Did fill the new-made world with light " ?

Is it fanciful to note that we have here, no
doubt in their barest primitive form, two of
Milton's life-long themes ?   The Authorized
Version speaks of " him that made great
lights " : how Miltonically transformed those
words already are in the two quoted lines !
De Quincey said that Milton was " not an
author amongst authors, not a poet amongst
poets, but a power amongst powers."   However that may be, it is certain that he, so
occupied all his life with thinking and writing
about God, thought of God habitually as a
power.   For him God is Creator, Sovereign,
Judge, much more often than Father : we
hear from Milton more of his might than of
his love.   So at once here, at the age of
fifteen, he inserts into the Psalm he is para-
phrasing that characteristic phrase, so splendid and potent itself, so gladly speaking of
potency and splendour,

" Who by his all-commanding might."

And, if power be one of the most frequent
elements in the Miltonic thought, what is more
frequent than light in the Miltonic vision ? And
is not that substitution of " did fill the new-
made world with light " for the bare scientific
statement of the original, a foretaste of the
Milton who, all his life, blind or seeing, felt

the joy and wonder of light as no other man ever did? Do we not rightly hear in it a note that will soon be enriched into the " Light unsufferable " of the *Ode*, the "endless morn of Light" of the *Solemn Music*, the " bosom bright of blazing Majesty and Light " of the *Epitaph on Lady Winchester*, and, not to multiply quotations, of the " Hail, holy Light" which opens the great invocation of the third book of *Paradise Lost*?

It may be as well, before discussing the *Ode* and the other contents of the volume issued in 1645, to mention another poem which is of earlier date than the *Ode*, though it was not printed till 1673: the beautiful Spenserian lines *On the Death of a Fair Infant*. They afford the most real of the exceptions to the rule that Milton is always from the beginning to the end unmistakably and solely himself. In this poem he shows himself at the age of seventeen so soaked in Spenser and Spenser's school that, when his baby niece dies and he sets himself to make her an elegy, what he gives us is these graceful verses conveying as much as a boy of seventeen can catch of the lovely elegiac note of Spenser.

" O noble Spirit : live there ever blessed
　The world's late wonder, and the heaven's
　　　new joy;

D

Live ever there, and leave me here distressed
With mortal cares and cumbrous world's
    annoy."

So sings Spenser of Sidney : and, though Milton
is scarcely yet more the equal of Spenser than
his baby niece was of Sidney, it is a beautiful
echo of his master that he gives us in his

" O fairest flower, no sooner blown but blasted,
Soft silken primrose fading timelessly,"

and in

" Yet can I not persuade me thou art dead,
    Or that thy corse corrupts in earth's dark
        womb,
    Or that thy beauties lie in wormy bed,
    Hid from the world in a low delvèd tomb."

The poem is full of the then fashionable
conceits, which appear again a little in the
Ode, after which they are for ever put aside by
Milton's imaginative severity and high conception of poetry as a finer sort of truth than
prose, not a more ingenious kind of lying.
Once, and perhaps once only, one hears in it
the voice of the Milton of later years—

" Thereby to set the hearts of men on fire
To scorn the sordid world, and unto Heaven
    aspire."

But with the *Ode* the age of imitation is
over for Milton and he stands forward at once

as himself. The soft graces, somewhat lacking in outline, of the *Fair Infant*, are forgotten in the sonorous strength of the *Ode*. The half-hesitating whisper has become a strain of mighty music; the uncertain hand has gained self-confidence so that the design now shows the boldness and decision of a master. At once, in the second stanza, he is away to heaven, with a curious anticipation of what was to occupy him so much thirty years later—

" That glorious form, that light unsufferable,
And that far-beaming blaze of majesty,
Wherewith he wont at Heaven's high council-
     table
To sit the midst of Trinal Unity,
He laid aside; and, here with us to be,
    Forsook the courts of everlasting day,
And chose with us a darksome house of
    mortal clay."

Milton's genius was universal, in the strict sense of the word, that is, living in or occupied with the universe. He is as supramundane in his way as Shelley in his. And no part of the universe was more real to him than heaven, the abode of God and angels and spirits, the original and ultimate home of his beloved music and light. It is noticeable that there is hardly a single poem of his — *L'Allegro* and *Samson* are the only important ones—in

which he does not at one point or other make
his escape to heaven. In most of them, as
all through this *Ode* and the *Solemn Music*,
in the conclusions of *Lycidas* and *Il Penseroso*,
in the opening of *Comus*, this heavenly flight
provides passages of exceptional and peculiarly Miltonic beauty. The fact is that,
though little of a mystic, he was from the
first entirely of that temper, intellectually
descended from Plato, morally from Stoicism
and Christianity but more from Stoicism,
which cannot be content to be " confined and
pestered in this pinfold here," disdains the
" low-thoughted cares " of mere bodily and
temporal life, and habitually aspires to live
the life of the mind and the spirit,

" Above the smoke and stir of this dim spot
    Which men call Earth."

So here at once, in his first important poem,
what in other hands might have been a mere
telling of the old human and earthly story of
the first Christmas night becomes in Milton's
a vision of all time and all space, with heaven
in it, and the stars, and the music of the
spheres, and the great timeless scheme of
redemption with which he was to have so
much to do later, with history, too, and literature, the false gods of the Old Testament
and of the Greek and Roman classics already

anticipating the parts they were to play in *Paradise Lost*.

And note one other thing. Milton is only twenty-one, but he is already an incomparable artist. The stanza had been so far the usual form for lyrics, and he adopts it here for the first and last time. But if he accepts the instrument prescribed by tradition, with what a master's hand this wonderful boy of twenty-one touches it, and to what astonishing music ! It seems that the stanza itself is his own. Every one has felt the combination in it, as he manages it, of the romantic movement and suggestion which he loved and renounced with the classical strength which is the chief element in the final impression he made on English poetry. As yet the romantic quality is the stronger, and even one of the mighty closing Alexandrines is dedicated to the lovely Elizabethan fancy of the " yellow skirted fayes " who

> " Fly after the night-steeds, leaving their
>   moon-loved maze."

How such a line as that, or still more plainly the two which end the most romantic stanza of all—

> " No nightly trance, or breathèd spell,
>   Inspires the pale-eyed priest from the
>   prophetic cell "

found a rejoicing echo in Keats is obvious.
This, of course, has often been noticed. But
has it ever been remarked that there are also
lines in the poem which might have been
written by another nineteenth-century poet
of equal but very different genius ?

> " The winds, with wonder whist,
>   Smoothly the waters kissed,
> Whispering new joys to the mild Ocean ; "—

should we be surprised to come upon these
elemental loves and joys heralding a new
reign of justice and peace in the *Prometheus
Unbound* ?

But neither Keats nor Shelley, who both
had their affinities to Milton, had it in him
to reach the concentrated Miltonic energy of
such lines as—

> " The wakeful trump of doom must thunder
>   through the deep,"

or—

> " Than his bright throne or burning axletree
>   could bear."

Almost every one of these final Alexandrines, it is to be observed, sums up the
note of its stanza in a chord of majestic
power. They are the most Miltonic lines
in the poem; for it is precisely " majesty "

which is the unique and essential Miltonic quality; and Dryden in the famous epigram ought to have kept it for him and not given it to Virgil, though by doing so he would have made his splendid compliment impossible.

Among the poems that followed in the 1645 edition were the *Passion*, a failure which Milton recognized as a failure and abandoned, but yet, characteristically, did not refuse to publish; the *Epitaph on the Marchioness of Winchester*, which, still youthful as it is and is seen to be by the frigid and false antithesis of Queen and Marchioness with which it ends, has yet very beautiful lines—

> " Gentle Lady, may thy grave
> Peace and quiet ever have !
> After this thy travail sore,
> Sweet rest seize thee evermore ";

the famous lines on Shakspeare, contributed anonymously to the second Folio; and the noble outburst of heavenly music which begins—

> " Blest pair of Sirens, pledges of Heaven's
>   joy
> Sphere-born harmonious sisters, Voice and
>   Verse."

This was written some years later; and
even after *Paradise Lost* it may rank as the
most daring and entirely successful of Milton's
long-sustained wheelings of musical flight.
The stanza no longer provides him with space
enough : and here his whole twenty-eight
lines are one continuous strain, with no
break in them and scarcely any pause, in
ten-syllabled lines of boldly varied rhyme
and accent.   His task here is not so difficult
as it was to be in *Paradise Lost*, for he has
rhyme to provide him with variety and he
admits two verses of six syllables among his
twenty-eight; but already he is completely
master of the possibilities of the ten-syllable
line, and can make it yield as lavish a wealth
of variety in unity as was later on to make
the great passages of *Paradise Lost* an eternal
amazement to lovers and practisers of the art
of verse.

" Wed your divine sounds, and mixed power
        employ,
    Dead things with inbreathed sense able to
        pierce ;
    And to our high-raised phantasy present
    That undisturbèd song of pure concent."

They are all the same line, and yet how
different.   It is difficult to believe that this
is the same metre which Waller and Dryden

were soon, amid universal applause, to file down into the smooth monotony of—

" Great wits are sure to madness near allied,
  And thin partitions do their bounds divide;
  Else why should he, with wealth and honour
      blest,
  Refuse his age the needful hours of rest ? "

For Dryden, as still more for Pope and the school of Pope, the thing to accomplish, so far as possible, is to prevent any strong natural accents falling upon the third, fifth or other odd syllables; there is, for instance, not one which does so in the first fifty lines of *Absalom and Achitophel* or of the *Epistle to Arbuthnot*. The object of Milton, on the contrary, is to vary the position of his accents to the utmost possible extent compatible with the preservation of the verse. In these four lines his first accent falls on the first syllable in the first two, probably on the fourth in the third, and on the second in the last. And the other accents are similarly varied in place and, it may be added, in number. In Milton's case the listener's wonder is at the number and intricacy of the variations he can play upon the theme of his verse; in Pope's it is at the amazing cleverness with which it can be exactly repeated in

D 2

different words. Milton's music, too, is continuous, not broken into couplets sharply divided from each other. His verses pass into each other as wave melts into wave on the sea-shore; there is a constant breaking on the beach, but which will break and which will glide imperceptibly into its successor we cannot guess though we sit watching for an hour; the sameness of rise and fall, crash and silence, is unbroken, yet no one wave is exactly like its predecessor, no two successive minutes give either eye or ear exactly the same experience. So with Milton's verse; even the ocean of *Paradise Lost* has few or no waves of music of more varied unity, of more continuous variety than such lines as—

" As once we did, till disproportioned sin
    Jarred against Nature's chime and with
       harsh din
    Broke the fair music that all creatures
       made
    To their great Lord, whose love their motion
       swayed
    In perfect diapason whilst they stood
    In first obedience and their state of good."

The chief remaining minor poems of Milton are the *Allegro* and *Penseroso, Comus, Lycidas* and the Sonnets. The two first are written

in those rhymed eight-syllable lines which he
had already used in part of his *Song on May
Morning*. Like that beautiful little poem,
they represent him in his simplest mood, the
mood of the quiet years at Horton, spent,
more than any other part of his life, in the
open air, and among plain folk unlettered and
unpolitical. It is natural enough, therefore,
that they are the most popular as they
are the easiest of all his poems. Their two
titles, which mean The Cheerful Man and
The Thoughtful or Meditative Man, point to
the two moods from which they regard life.
Both moods are, of course, described as
they might actually be experienced by a
highly cultivated and serious man like Milton
himself. The gravity is the gravity of a man
of thought, not of a man of affairs; the
pleasures are those of a scholar and a poet,
not those of a trifler, a sportsman, or a
sensualist. Like all Milton's works they
borrow freely from earlier poets, remain
entirely original and Miltonic, and are imitated only at the peril of the imitator. Any
one who looks at the parallel passages in
Marlowe and Fletcher will see how very like
they are and how very little the likeness
matters. The poems stand alone; there is
nothing of quite the same kind in English.

The least unlike pair of poems is perhaps the
two Spring Odes of the present Poet Laureate,
than whom no one has owed more to Milton
or repaid the debt with more verse which
Milton would have been glad to inspire.
But Mr. Bridges has, of course, avoided anything approaching a direct imitation; he has
merely used the hint of two contrasted poems
on one subject, touching inevitably, as Milton
had touched, upon some of the opposite
pleasures of town and country, and bringing
Milton's mood of cheerful gravity to bear
upon them both.

It is unnecessary to discuss in detail poems
so well known. But a few words may be
said. Milton was never again to be so genial
as he is here. Never again does he place
himself so sympathetically close to the daily
tasks and pleasures of ordinary unimportant
men and women. After characteristically
choosing the West Wind and the Dawn as
likelier parents of true mirth than any god
of wine or sensual pleasure, he will go on for
once to call for the company of—

" Sport that wrinkled Care derides,
    And Laughter holding both his sides ";

he will cast a pleased eye on the birds and
flowers and the sunrise—the latter moving

him to the characteristic magnificence which
in this poem he has elsewhere forgone; he
will recognize, with the gratefulness of the
tired student, the careless gladness in the
voices of ploughman and milkmaid, as he
passes them in his early morning walk. Then
he will give a glance to beauty which such as
they cannot see, or cannot be fully conscious
of seeing—

" Mountains on whose barren breast
  The labouring clouds do often rest ";

will touch on the romance of old towers and
poetic memories of which they have only
dimly heard, and look back at Thyrsis
and Corydon and all the pastoral poetry
which such scenes recall to the scholar's
memory. The next section of the poem is
taken from a different world, that of the
merry England of the Middle Age with its
ale and dances and Faery Mab; while the final
one carries us quite away from the rustics to
the town and the town's pleasures, pageantry
and drama and music—this last, as always,
moving the poet to peculiar rapture, and an
answering music of verse—

" The melting voice through mazes running,
  Untwisting all the chains that tie
  The hidden soul of harmony."

Il Penseroso is the praise of Melancholy as
L'Allegro of Mirth.   But Milton was not a
melancholy man in our sense of the word.
When Keats declares that—

> " in the very temple of Delight
> Veiled Melancholy has her sovran shrine,"

he is interpreting a mood into which Milton
could not even in imagination enter, that of
the intellectual sensualist who dreams his life
away and cannot act.   Milton was a man
of action and character, and his Melancholy,
quite unlike this, is that of the Spirit in his
own *Comus*, who " began—

> " Wrapt in a pleasing fit of melancholy,
> To meditate my rural minstrelsy."

He hails her at once as a " Goddess sage and
holy " and as a " Nun devout and pure ";
and it is evident from the first that her
sorrows, so far as she is sorrowful, are those
of aspiring spirit, not those of self-indulging
and disappointed flesh.   Her life of quiet
studies and pleasures is self-chosen; there is
a note of will and self-control in the words
in which the poet bids her call about her
Peace and Quiet and Spare Fast, Retired
Leisure and Contemplation and Silence; and
the descriptions which follow of his walks

and studies and pleasures, in town and country, by night and morning, are those of a man who has deliberately shaped his life, and means so to live it that he shall leave it without regret or shame and with the hope of passing from it to a better.

Nor is it any mood of mere melancholy that has given us in this poem such pleasant glimpses of his walks abroad and studies at home in these Horton years. He pays his tribute to Plato, the Greek tragedians and the dramatists of Elizabethan and Jacobean England; and to his own two most famous predecessors, Chaucer and Spenser; and we think of the scholarly hours spent gravely and quietly but far from unhappily. More delightful still, with more beauty and more happiness in them, are the poem's well-known landscapes—

> " the wandering moon,
> Riding near her highest noon,
> Like one that had been led astray
> Through the heaven's wide pathless way."

Perhaps no one again, till Shelley came, felt the vastness, the pathlessness, of the heaven as Milton did. Or, to come to earth again, where does poetry set the ear more instantly and actively at the work of imaginative

creation than in those finely suggestive lines
about the curfew—

> " Over some wide-watered shore,
> Swinging slow with sullen roar " ?

And what of that woodland solitude at
noon, with memories in it of so many poets
of Greece, Rome, Italy and England, the

> " shadows brown, that Sylvan loves,
> Of pine, or monumental oak,
> Where the rude axe with heavèd stroke
> Was never heard the Nymphs to daunt
> Or fright them from their hallowed haunt,"

which carries us on to perhaps the loveliest
lines in all the *Paradise Lost*—

> ." In shadier bower,
> More sacred and sequestered, though but
> feigned,
> Pan or Sylvanus never slept, nor nymph
> Nor Faunus haunted."

There is in the two passages just the difference
between the youth and maturity of genius;
but that is all. So *Il Penseroso* passes on its
delightful way, ending, of course, in music
and heaven.

There, too, " before the starry threshold
of Jove's court," the next of these earlier
works of Milton, the mask *Comus*, begins.

It strikes its high note at once in what an
old lover of literature boldly called "the
finest opening of any theatrical piece ancient
or modern."

" Before the starry threshold of Jove's court
  My mansion is, where those immortal
    shapes
Of bright aerial spirits live insphered
In regions mild of calm and serene air,
Above the smoke and stir of this dim spot
 Which men call Earth, and, with low-
    thoughted care,
Confined and pestered in this pinfold here,
Strive to keep up a frail and feverish being,
Unmindful of the crown that Virtue gives,
After this mortal change, to her true
    servants
Amongst the enthron'd gods on sainted
    seats."

That looks forward to *Paradise Lost*, not
backward to the masks of the previous
generation of poets. The "loud uplifted
angel-trumpet" is sounded in it, and we
know that we have travelled a long way from
the trivial, superficial and often coarse entertainments which would have been the models
of *Comus* if Milton had not been the last man
to accept models of any kind, and especially
of that kind. Like them his mask was an
aristocratic entertainment, played to a noble

audience by the scions of a great house.
But the resemblance scarcely goes further.
The older masks were mainly spectacles;
magnificent spectacles indeed, designed sometimes, as one may see in the Chatsworth
Library, by such artists as Inigo Jones and
produced at immense expense; but just for
that reason addressed to the eye much more
than to the ear, and scarcely at all to the
mind. Even when written by such a man as
Ben Jonson, the words, except in the lyrics,
are of almost no importance. The business
was to show a number of pretty scenes, and
noble ladies, and to give them a chance of
exhibiting their clothes, and their voices.
The last gave Jonson his chance; the fine
Horatian workman that he was could always
produce a lyric that would fit any situation
and give some dignity to any trivial person-
age. But the taint of vanity and fashion,
pomp and externality, inevitably clung to
the whole thing. Too many personages were
introduced, probably because in such plays
there were always a great many applicants
for parts; and the inevitable result was that
in a short piece none of them had space to
develop any character or life. But Milton
knew, as the Greeks knew and Shakspeare
did not always, that in the few hours of a

stage performance only a very few characters
have time to develop themselves in such a
way as to interest and convince the hearer's
imagination, and that if there are many they
never become more than a list of names. So
he, who could not touch anything without
giving it character, limits his personages to
four or five that they may at least be human
beings and not mere singers of songs or
allegorical abstractions. And, like some of
his predecessors, he takes an ethical theme,
the praise and power of Chastity. Fletcher
in *The Faithful Shepherdess* had taken the
same; as Jonson had taken the praise of
Temperance, which is also partly Milton's
subject, in *Pleasure Reconciled to Virtue*, in
which a grosser Comus is one of the characters. But to get any parallel to the power
of conviction with which Milton handles it
one has to go behind Jonson, whose mask is
an entirely superficial performance, and even
behind Fletcher, in whose *Shepherdess* the
many beautiful and moving touches are lost
in a crowd of characters and a wilderness of
artificial intrigue; one has to go back to the
man whom Milton once called his " original,"
to the author of the *Faerie Queen*. No one
but Spenser could have anticipated the scene
between Comus and the Lady, where indeed

Milton, like Spenser in the bower of Acrasia, has lavished such wealth upon his sinner that he has hardly been able to give a due over-balance to his saint. Yet she is no lay figure, and one is not surprised that Comus should twice show his consciousness that she has within her some holy, some more than mortal power. Milton has given her a song of such astonishing music that one wonders whether the composer Lawes, for whom the whole was written, could touch it without injury—

" Sweet Echo, sweetest Nymph, that liv'st
　　　　unseen
　　　Within thy airy shell
　　By slow Meander's margent green,
　And in the violet-embroidered vale
　　Where the love-lorn nightingale
　Nightly to thee her sad song mourneth
　　　　well;
　Canst thou not tell me of a gentle pair
　　　That likest thy Narcissus are ?
　　　　O, if thou have
　　　Hid them in some flowery cave,
　　　　Tell me but where,
　　Sweet Queen of Parley, Daughter of the
　　　　Sphere !
　So mayst thou be translated to the skies,
　And give resounding grace to all Heaven's
　　　harmonies."

The lyrics were the chief beauty of the old masks, but the best of them sink into in-

significance before such a masterpiece of art
as this. Perhaps nothing in a modern language
comes nearer to giving the peculiar effect
which is the glory of Pindar. Of course there
is in it more of the fanciful, and more of the
romantic, than there was in Pindar; and its
style is tenderer, prettier and perhaps altogether smaller than his. But the elaborate
and intricate perfection of its art and language,
the way in which the intellect in it serves the
imagination, is exactly Pindar. In any case it
is certainly one of the most entirely beautiful
of English lyrics. One listens with delight
to the musician working out his intricately
beautiful theme; or is it nearer the impression
we get to say that we watch the skilful dancer
executing his elaborate figure? In either case
we await with sure confidence the triumphant
close. The final couplet, by the way, and particularly the great Alexandrine, is a curious
anticipation of Dryden's finest manner. But
the rest is a music Dryden's ear never heard.
No wonder Comus cries—

" Can any mortal mixture of earth's mould
   Breathe such divine enchanting ravishment?
   Sure something holy lodges in that breast,
   And with these raptures moves the vocal
      air
   To testify his hidden residence.

How sweetly did they float upon the wings
Of silence, through the empty-vaulted night,
At every fall smoothing the raven down
Of darkness till it smiled ! "

The last lines show that Milton has not yet outgrown the Jacobean taste for conceits. So a little later on we find him writing that—

" Silence
Was took ere she was ware, and wished she
    might
Deny her nature, and be never more
Still to be so displaced " ;

a piece of intellectual trickery such as Shakspeare too often played with, and Donne laboured at; and one of a special interest because we see it again later transformed and purified in the famous passage of *Paradise Lost*, in which " Silence was pleased " not only with the stillness of evening, but also with the song of the bird whose "amorous descant " alone interrupts it. Yet even that seemed to Warton, the best of Milton's early critics, a conceit unworthy of the poet. So difficult it is for " rational " criticism to see the distinction between an intellectual extravagance and a flight of the imagination.

There are other things in *Comus* beside conceits which recall Shakspeare. What can

be more exactly in his freshest youngest
manner than such a line as—

"Love-darting eyes and tresses like the
        morn"?

And what can be closer to the note of the
great Histories and Tragedies than the Elder
Brother's outburst of faith—

                "If this fail,
    The pillared firmament is rottenness,
    And earth's base built on stubble"?

I see no reason whatever to doubt, in
spite of what has lately been said by a
modern critic and poet, that these speeches
of the Brothers and the Lady, rather than
those of Comus, represent Milton's own conception of life.   It is true, of course, that
Comus was one of several masks performed
as an aristocratic counterblast to the attack
of Prynne and the Puritans on all stage
performances.   But that only strengthens the
proof of Milton's own leaning to a grave and
temperate mode of life.   Even when he writes
a mask he will insist that it shall be a thing
of noble art and serious moral.   He was no
narrow-minded fanatic and will write a piece
for great ladies to perform when asked by his
accomplished friend Lawes : but he is already

the man who was later to denounce " court amours, Mix'd dance and wanton masque "; and if he writes a mask himself it will be to take the old " high-flown commonplace " of the magic power of chastity and give it an entirely new-.seriousness and beauty. The notion of Mr. Newbolt that there were two Miltons, one before and the other after the Civil War, and that the one was " sincerely engaged on the side of liberal manners " while the other was an ill-tempered enemy of civilization and the arts of life, is a complete delusion. The " lady of Christ's " who was unpopular on account of his severe chastity, was already a strict Puritan of the only sort he ever became; and the author of *Paradise Lost*, as all the evidence shows, was no morbid sectary but a lover of learning and music and society. Of course, no man goes unchanged through a great struggle such as that to which Milton gave twenty years of life. There is a development, or a difference, call it what you will, between the Dante who wrote the *Vita Nuova* and him who wrote the *Divina Commedia*. That could not but be; a body that had gone into exile and a soul that had visited hell must leave their traces on a man. But the essential Dante remains one and the same all the while. And

so does Milton.   Nothing can be more certain
than that the grave boy whose gravity im-
pressed all Cambridge, and had taken immortal
shape in the *Nativity Ode* and the sonnet of
the " great Taskmaster's eye " before he was
much past twenty, did not mean to hold up a
drunken sensualist like Comus as a model for
youth.   He was not an ascetic, then or later;
and he was writing a dramatic poem; and,
of course, had no difficulty in giving Comus a
fine speech about the follies of total abstinence
which, indeed, he loved no better than other
monkeries.   The Lady, in reply, as she is
dramatically bound, over-exalts her " sage
and serious doctrine of Virginity " as Comus
had overstated the case against it; but what
she praises is Temperance, not Abstinence.
Her virginity is that of a free maiden, not that
of a vowed nun, and there is nothing in it to
unfit her to play the part which, when Eve
plays it, gives Milton occasion for his well-
known apostrophe to true love.   Nor is there
any inconsistency between his denunciation
of " wanton masks " in that passage, and his
being the author of *Comus*.   His own mask
was as different as possible from those others,
the common sort, in which he saw the pur-
veyors of " adulterous lust," and with which,
now as then, he would have nothing whatever

to do. His " Lady " alone, even without her
brothers, makes that clear. What she says
may not be so poetically attractive as the
speech of Comus ; but it has just the note of
exaltation which is heard in all Milton's great
ethical and spiritual outbursts, and plainly
utters the other and stronger side of his con-
victions. The truth is that from the very
beginning to the very end of his life Milton
had all the intensity of Puritanism, more
than all its angry contempt of vice, but
nothing whatever of its uncivilized narrow-
mindedness. A large part of the peculiar
interest of his character lies in the fact that
he, almost alone of Englishmen, managed to
unite the strength of the Reformation with the
breadth of the Renaissance. We have both
in the lovely verses which are the Epilogue
of *Comus ;* and if it begins with—

> " the gardens fair
> Of Hesperus, and his daughters three
> That sing about the golden tree : "

and the—

> " Beds of hyacinth and roses
> Where young Adonis oft reposes,
> Waxing well of his deep wound
> In slumber soft, and on the ground
> Sadly sits the Assyrian queen " ;

it ends with the Stoic Puritan motto, " Love
Virtue, she alone is free."   And that these
last six lines were no formal compliment to
the conventions is proved by the fact that
Milton chose the final couplet—

> " if Virtue feeble were
> Heaven itself would stoop to her,"

as the motto he appended to his signature in
the album of an Italian Protestant at Geneva
in 1639, adding the significant Latin which
claims the sentiment as utterly his own—

" Cælum, non animum, muto dum trans mare
    curro."

These words we, looking back on his whole
life, may fitly translate : " I am always the
same John Milton, whether in Rome, Geneva,
or London, whether I write *Comus* or *Allegro*
or *Paradise Lost*."   For never were unity and
continuity of personality more complete than
in Milton.

There remains *Lycidas,* in which Milton out-
distances all previous English elegy almost as
easily as in *Comus* he had out-distanced all
the earlier masks.   It stands with the great
passages of *Paradise Lost* as the most consummate blending of scholarship and poetry
in Milton and therefore in English.   All

pastoral poetry is in it, Theocritus and
Virgil, Spenser and Sidney, Drayton and
Drummond, with memories, too, of Ovid
and Shakspeare and the Bible; and yet it
is pure and undiluted Milton, with the signet
of his peculiar mind and temper stamped on
its every phrase. It was his contribution to
a volume of verses published at Cambridge
in 1638 to the memory of Edward King, a
younger contemporary of his at Christ's who
was drowned off the Welsh coast in August
1637. King was already a Fellow of his
college, and one of the most promising young
clergymen of his day. Milton had liked and
respected him, no doubt, but had certainly
not been so intimate with him as with young
Charles Diodati who died almost exactly a
year later, and was lamented by his great
friend in the *Epitaphium Damonis* which is
the finest of the Latin poems. Those who
read Latin will enjoy its close parallelism
with *Lycidas* and its touches of a still closer
bond of affection, as that in which the poet
contrasts the easy friendships of birds and
animals, soon won, soon lost and soon replaced by others, with their hard rareness
among men who scarcely find one kindred
spirit in a thousand, and too often lose that
one by premature fate before the fruit of

friendship has had time to ripen. But if the death of Diodati aroused the deeper sorrow in Milton, that of King produced unquestionably the greater poem. It is a common mistake to think that to write a great elegy a man must have suffered a great sorrow. That is not the case. Shelley wrote *Adonais* about Keats whom he knew very little; Spenser *Daphnaïda* about a lady whom he did not know at all. It is not the actual experience of sorrow that the elegiac poet needs; but the power of heart and imagination to conceive it and the power of language to give it fit expression. Moreover, the poet's real subject is not the death of Keats or King or Mrs. Gorges : it is the death of all who have been or will be loved in all the world, and the sorrow of all the survivors, the tragic destiny of youth and hope and fame, the doom of frailty and transience which has been eternally pronounced on so many of the fairest gifts of Nature and all the noblest works of man.

About *Lycidas* criticism has less to say than to unsay. Johnson's notorious attack upon it is only the extremest instance of the futility of applying to poetry the tests of prose and of the general incapacity of that generation to apply any other. Even

Warton, who really loved these early poems
of Milton and did so much to recall them to
public notice, could speak of him as appearing
to have had " a very bad ear " ! At such a
time it was inevitable that the artificial
absurdity of pastoral poetry which is a prose
fact should blind all but the finest judges to
the poetic fact that living spirit can animate
every form it finds prepared for its indwelling.
Johnson and the rest were right in perceiving
that pastoral elegy had very commonly been
an insincere affectation, a mere exercise
in writing; the age into which they were
born denied them the ear that could hear
the amazing music of *Lycidas*, or perceive
the sensuous, imaginative, spiritual intensity
which drowns its incongruities in a flood of
poetic life. There is a still more important
truth which that generation could not see.
Prose aims at expressing facts directly, and
sometimes succeeds. That is what Johnson
liked, and practised himself with masterly
success. But when he and his asked that
poetry should do the same they were asking
that she should deny her nature. She knows
that her truth can only be expressed or suggested by its imaginative equivalents. It is
with poetry as with religion. Religious truth
stated directly becomes philosophy or science,

conveying other elements of truth, perhaps, but failing to convey the element which is specifically religious; and therefore religion employs parable, ceremony, sacrament, mystery, to express what scientifically exact prose cannot express. So poetry can neither deal directly with King's death or Milton's grief nor be content with a subject which is a mere fact in time and space. If it did, the effect produced would not be a poetic effect; the experience of the reader would not be a poetic experience. The poet must transform or transcend the facts which have set his powers to work; he must escape from them or rather lift them up with him new-created into the world of the imagination; he must impose upon them a new form, invented or accepted by himself, and in any case so heated by his own fire of poetry that it can fuse and reshape the matter submitted to it into that unity of beauty which is a work of art. That is what Milton does in *Lycidas* by the help of the pastoral fiction; and what he could not have done without it or some imaginative substitute for it.

The truest criticism on his pastoralism is really that that mould was too small and fragile to hold all he wanted to put into it. The great outburst of St. Peter, with its scarcely disguised assault upon the Laudian clergy, strains it almost to bursting. Yet no one would wish it away; for it adds a passage of Miltonic fire to what but for Phœbus and St. Peter would be too plaintive to be fully characteristic of Milton whose genius lay rather in strength than in tenderness. Yet perhaps we love *Lycidas* all the more for giving us our almost solitary glimpse of a Milton in whom the affections are more than the will, and sorrow not sublimated into resolution. Its modesty, too, is astonishing. He had already written the *Nativity Ode*, *Comus* and *Allegro* and *Penseroso*, and yet he fancies himself still unripe for poetry and is only forced by the " bitter constraint " of the death of his friend to pluck the berries of his laurel which seem to him still " harsh and crude "; for of course these allusions refer to his own immaturity and not, as Todd thought, to that of his dead friend. And the presence of the same over-mastering emotion which compelled him to begin is felt throughout. There is no poem of his in which he appears to make so complete a surrender to the changing moods of passion. The verses seem to follow his heart and fancy just where they choose to lead. We watch him as he thinks first of his friend's death and then of the duty of paying some poetic tribute to him; and so of his own death and of some other poet of the future who may write of it and—

" bid fair peace be to my sable shroud."

How natural it is in all its superficial un-naturalness ! The walks and talks and verses made together at Cambridge so inevitably leading to the " heavy change now thou art gone, Now thou art gone and never must return "; and the fancy, partly but not wholly a reminiscence of their classical studies, that the trees and flowers which they had loved together must now be sharing the survivor's grief; the reproach to Nature and Nature's divinities following on the thought of Nature's sympathy, and followed by the first of the two incomparable returns upon himself which are among the chief beauties of the poem—

" Ay me !   I fondly dream !
 ' Had ye been there,' for what could that
        have done ? "

And so to the vanity of earthly fame and the thought of another fame which is not vanity. Twice he seems to be going to escape out of the world of pastoral, as he strikes his own trumpet note of confident

E

faith and stern judgment; twice the unfailing
instinct of art calls him back and makes a
beauty of what might have been a mere
incongruity—

" Return, Alpheus; the dread voice is past, .
    That shrunk thy streams : return, Sicilian
        Muse,
    And call the vales, and bid them hither cast
    Their bells and flowerets of a thousand
        hues."

The flowers come, in their amazing beauty, as
poetry knows and names them, not altogether
after the order of nature; till the fine flight
is once more recalled to earth in that second
return to the sad reality of things which
provides the most beautiful, and as the
manuscript shows, one of the most carefully
elaborated passages in the whole—

" Bid amaranthus all his beauty shed,
    And daffadillies fill their cups with tears,
    To strew the laureate hearse where Lycid
        lies.
    For so, to interpose a little ease,
    Let our frail thoughts dally with false
        surmise.
    Ay me ! whilst thee the shores and sounding
        seas
    Wash far away, where'er thy bones are
        hurled,
    Whether beyond the stormy Hebrides,

Where thou perhaps under the whelming
   tide
Visit'st the bottom of the monstrous world."

The least critical reader, when he is told
that the daffodil and amaranthus lines were
once in the reverse order, that the " frail
thoughts " were at first " sad," and the
" shores " " floods," and above all that the
" whelming tide " was once a thing so insignificant as the " humming tide," can judge
for himself by what a succession of inspira-
tions a work of consummate art is produced.

There remain the sonnets, whose sufficient
praise is given in an immortal line of Wordsworth, while all that a fine critic had thought
or learnt about them is contained in the
scholarly edition of Mark Pattison. Techni-
cally they are remarkable, like everything else
of Milton's, at once for their conservatism
and their originality; while their content has
all his characteristic sincerity. They occupy
a most important place in the history of the
English sonnet, which had so far been almost
entirely given up to a single theme, that of
the poet's unhappy love, which had commonly little existence outside his verses. The
shadowy mistresses who emulated the glories
of Beatrice and Laura were even less sub-
stantial than they; and, though that could

not hinder great poets from making fine poetry out of them, it was fatal to the ordinary sonnetteer, and gave the sonnet a tradition of overblown and insincere verbiage. From all this Milton emancipated it and, as Landor said, "gave the notes to glory." To glory and to other things; for not all his sonnets are consecrated to glory. They deal with various subjects; but each, whether its topic be his blindness, the death of his wife, or the fame of Fairfax or Cromwell, is the product of a personal experience of his own. No one can read them through without feeling that he gets from them a true knowledge of the man. At their weakest, as in that *To a Lady*, they convey, in the words of Mark Pattison, "the sense that here is a true utterance of a great soul." The rather commonplace thought and language somehow do not prevent the total effect from being impressive. He entirely fails only when he goes below the level of poetry altogether and repeats in verse the angry scurrility of his divorce pamphlets. And even there some remnant of his artist's sense of the self-restraint of verse preserves him from the worst degradations of his prose. For the rest, they give us his musical and scholarly tastes, his temperate pleasures and his love of that sort of company which Shelley confessed to preferring, "such society as is quiet, wise and good"; they give us the high ideal with which he became a poet, the high patriotism that drew him into politics, and that sense, both for himself and for others, of life as a thing to be lived in the presence and service of God which was the eternally true part of his religion. The four finest are those on the Massacre in Piedmont, On his Blindness, On attaining the age of twenty-three, and that addressed to Cromwell, which perhaps has the finest touch of all in the pause which comes with such tremendous effect after "And Worcester's laureate wreath." But that to the memory of his wife and "Captain or Colonel or Knight in Arms," the one addressed to Lawrence and the first of those addressed to Skinner, come very near the best; and the whole eight would be included by any good judge in a collection of the fifty best English sonnets, to which Milton would make a larger contribution than any one except, perhaps, Wordsworth and Shakspeare.

And both of these poets, Shakspeare always and Wordsworth often, sinned as Milton did not against the true genius of the sonnet. No doubt they nearly all had precedent in their favour, perhaps most of their successors

have followed in the same path. But not
even Shakespeare and Petrarch can alter the
fact that the genius of the sonnet is solitary
and self-contained. A series of sonnets is
an artistic contradiction in terms. There
may be magnificent individual sonnets in
it which can stand alone, without reference
to those that precede or follow; and so far
so good; but on the bulk of the series there
inevitably rests the taint of incompleteness.
They do not explain themselves. They are
chapters not books, parts of a composition
and not the whole. It is scarcely possible to
doubt that, fine as they may be, the effect
they produce is not that of the finest single
sonnets, beginning and ending within their
own limits. Milton may never have been
under any special temptation to write a set
of consecutive sonnets; but it is in any case
like his habitual submission of all authority
to his own judgment that he wrote sonnets
and yet defied the tradition of writing them
as a continuous series, as he had also disdained
the amorous affectations which had been their
established subject. But in this, as in everything else where art was concerned, he was
as much a conservative as a revolutionary.
And so his scholarly interest in the Italian
sonnet, and, we may be sure, his consummate

critical judgment, made him set aside the
various sonnet forms adopted by Shakspeare,
Spenser and other famous English poets, and
follow the original model of Petrarch more
strictly than it had been followed by any
English poet of importance before him; for
the Petrarchan sonnets of Sidney, Constable
and Drummond all end with the unItalian
concluding couplet. But here again Milton's
example has not proved decisive. Wordsworth did not always follow it, though he
never deserted it with success. Keats began
with it and gave it up for the Shakspearean
model with the concluding couplet. But of
him again, it may be said that, while he only
wrote three great sonnets and two of them
are Shakspearean, his single masterpiece is
Petrarchan or Miltonic. Rossetti, on the
other hand, has no Shakspearean sonnets, and
his finest are among the best proofs of how
much a sonnet gains in unity by the single
pause between the eight lines and the six
instead of Shakspeare's fourfold division, and
especially by the interlocking of the rhymes in
the second half of the sonnet as opposed to
Shakspeare's isolated and half-epigrammatic
final couplet.

There can be little doubt, though attempts
have been made to deny it, that nothing but

the prestige of the greatest of all poetic
names has prevented the superiority of the
Petrarchan model from being universally
recognized. Shakspeare could do anything.
But the greatness of his sonnets is due not to
their form but simply to their being his; and
the fact that he could triumph over the
defects of that form ought not to make other
people fancy that these defects do not exist.
They do; and but for the courage and genius
of Milton they might have dominated the
history of the English sonnet to this day.
That is part of our great debt to Milton. He
could not give the sonnet the supple and
insinuating sweetness with which Shakspeare
often filled it. He had not got that in him,
and perhaps it would scarcely have proved
tolerable except as part of a sequence in
which it could be balanced by sterner matter.
Nor, again, could he give it Shakspeare's
infinite tenderness, nor his sense of the world's
brooding mystery. But he could and did
give it his own high spirit of courage, sincerity
and strength, and his own masterly cunning
of craftsmanship. And no just reader of the
greatest sonnets of the nineteenth century
forgets Milton's share in their greatness. Mr.
Lascelles Abercrombie has lately remarked
that it is in the *Prelude* and *Excursion* of

Wordsworth that " more profoundly than anywhere out of Milton himself Milton's spiritual legacy is employed." The same thing may be as truly said of Wordsworth's sonnets. If, as he said, in Milton's hands " the thing became a trumpet," there is no doubt that it remained one in his own. He is a greater master of the sonnet than Milton; the greatest on the whole that England has known. He used it far more freely than Milton and for more varied purposes. Perhaps it hardly afforded room enough for one the peculiar note of whose genius was vastness. It is seldom possible to do justice to a quotation from *Paradise Lost* without giving at least twenty lines. The sense, and especially the musical effect, is incomplete with less; for a Miltonic period is a series of intellectual and rhythmical actions and reactions which cannot be detached from each other without loss. It is obvious that a poet whose natural range is so great can hardly be fully himself in the sonnet. But Wordsworth had little of this spacious freedom of poetic energy; to him—

" 'twas pastime to be bound
Within the sonnet's scanty plot of ground."

And so he could use it for everything; for great events and also for very small; not

E 2

exhausting great or small, but finding in each, whatever it might be, some single aspect or quality which he could touch to new power by that meditative tenderness of his to which Milton was, to his great loss, an entire stranger. The natural mysticism, for instance, of such sonnets as, " It is a beauteous evening, calm and free," or, " Earth has not anything to show more fair," is quite out of Milton's reach. In this and other ways Wordsworth could do much more with the sonnet than Milton could. But without Milton some of his very greatest things would scarcely have been attempted. All the sonnets that utter his magnanimous patriotism, his dauntless passion for English liberty, his burning sympathy with the oppressed, the "holy glee" of his hatred of tyranny, are of the right lineage of Milton himself. One can almost hear Milton crying—

" It is not to be thought of that the Flood
　Of British freedom, which to the open sea
　Of the world's praise from dark antiquity
　Hath flowed ' with pomp of waters unwith-
　　　stood,'
　Roused though it be full often to a mood
　Which spurns the checks of salutary bands,
　That this most famous Stream in Bogs and
　　　Sands
　Should perish; and to evil and to good
　Be lost for ever."

There and in the "Two Voices" and in the
"Inland within a Hollow Vale" and in the
Toussaint l'Ouverture sonnet, and others, we
cannot fail to catch an echo of the poet who
first "gave the sonnet's notes to glory."   No
one can count up all the things which have
united in the making of any poem, but among
those which made these sonnets possible must
certainly be reckoned the Fairfax and Cromwell sonnets, and above all the still more
famous one on the Massacre in Piedmont.
The forces which animated England to defy
and defeat Napoleon were only partly moral;
but so far as they were that they found perfect
expression through only one voice, that of
Wordsworth.   And there is no doubt as to
where he caught the note which he struck
again to such high purpose.   He has told us
himself—

"Milton, thou shouldst be living at this hour;
    England hath need of thee."

And, what seems stranger, he has now had
in return a kind of reflected influence upon
Milton.   The total experience of a reader of
poetry is a thing of many actions and reactions, co-operating and intermingling with
each other.   And as we can hardly read Virgil
or the Psalms now without thinking of all

that has come of them, and reading some of it
back into the old words whose first creator
could not foresee all that would be found in
them, so it is with Milton and Wordsworth.
There are many things in Milton which no
Wordsworthian can now read exactly as
they were read in the seventeenth century.
Wordsworth's line

" Thy Soul was like a Star and dwelt apart "

was strangely true of Milton as he lived in
his own day. But it is less true now that
his place is among the spiritual company
of the English poets and that Wordsworth
stands by his side, or sits at his feet. That
does not detract from his greatness. Indeed,
it adds to it; for it is only the greater poets
who thus transcend their own day and cannot
be read as if they belonged to it alone. Read
the great sonnet on the Massacre—

" Avenge, O Lord, thy slaughtered saints,
        whose bones
    Lie scattered on the Alpine mountains
        cold;
    Even them who kept thy truth so pure
        of old,
    When all our fathers worshiped stocks
        and stones,

Forget not; in thy book record their groans
  Who were thy sheep, and in their ancient
    fold
  Slain by the bloody Piemontese, that
    rolled
  Mother with infant down the rocks.
    Their moans
The vales redoubled to the hills, and they
  To heaven. Their martyred blood and
    ashes sow
  O'er all the Italian fields, where still doth
    sway
The triple Tyrant; that from these may
    grow
  A hundredfold, who, having learnt thy
    way,
Early may fly the Babylonian woe."

Is there not more in it than the Hebrew
prophet or psalmist and the English Puritan?
Is there not, for us now, something beside
the past of which Milton had read, and the
present which he knew by experience? Is
there not an anticipation of another struggle
against another tyrant—nay, the creation of
the very spirit in which that struggle was to
be faced? So Milton influences Wordsworth
and the England of Wordsworth's day; and
they in their turn inevitably influence our
minds as we read him. There lies one part of
the secret of his greatness; a part which is
seen at its highest in his sonnets.

CHAPTER IV

PARADISE LOST

PARADISE LOST is in several ways one of the most wonderful of the works of man. And not least in the circumstances of its composition. The Restoration found Milton blind, and to blindness it added disappointment, defeat, obscurity, and fear of the public or private revenge of his victorious enemies. Yet out of such a situation as this the most indomitable will that ever inhabited the soul of a poet produced three great poems, every one of which would have been enough to give him a place among the poets who belong to the whole world.

The first and greatest of these was, of course, *Paradise Lost.* Unlike many great poems, but like all the great epics of the world, it obtained recognition at once. It sold well for a work of its bulk and seriousness, and it received the highest praise from those whose word was and deserved to be law in questions of literature. Throughout the eighteenth

century its fame and popularity increased.
Literary people read it ,because Dryden and
Addison and all the established authorities
recommended it to them, and also because
those of them whose turn for literature was
a reality found that these recommendations
were confirmed by their own experience. But
the poem also appealed to another and a
larger public. To the serious world it appeared to be a religious book and as such
enjoyed the great advantage of being thought
fit to be read on the only day in the week on
which many people were accustomed to read
at all. This distinction grew in importance
with the progress of the Wesleyan revival and
with it grew the number of Milton's admirers.
When Sunday readers were tired of the Bible
they were apt to turn to *Paradise Lost.* How
many of them did so is proved by the influence
Milton has had on English religious beliefs.
To this day if an ordinary man is asked to
give his recollections of the story of Adam and
Eve he is sure to put Milton as well as Genesis
into them. For instance, the Miltonic Satan
is almost sure to take the place of the scriptural serpent. The influence Milton has had
is unfortunately also seen in less satisfactory
ways. He claimed to justify the ways of God
to men. Perhaps he did so to his own mind

which, in these questions, was curiously
matter-of-fact, literal, legal and unmystical.
He was determined to explain everything and
provide for all contingencies by his legal
instrument of the government of the world :
and he did so after the cold fashion of a
lawyer defining rights on each side, and assum-
ing that the stronger party will exert his
strength. So far as his genius made his
readers accept his views of the relation between God and man it cannot be denied that
he did a great injury to English religious
thought. Everybody who stops to reflect
now feels that the attitude of his God to the
rebel angels and to man is hard and unfor-
giving, below the standard of any decent
human morality, far below the Christian
charity of St. Paul. The atmosphere of the
poem when it deals with these matters is
often suggestive of a tyrant's attorney-
general whose business is to find plausible
excuses for an arbitrary despot. Milton had
his share in creating that bad sort of fear of
God which is always appearing as the thorn
in the theological rose-bed of the eighteenth
century, and, later on, becomes the night-
mare of the Evangelical revival. None of
these conceptions, the capricious despot, the
remorseless creditor, the Judge whose in-

variable sentence is hell fire, have proved easy to get rid of : and part of their permanence may be laid to the account of *Paradise Lost*.

But Milton, who is like the Bible in so many ways, is not least like it in his happy unconsciousness of his own immorality. The writer of the story of Samuel and Agag, or that of Rebekah and Jacob, was perfectly unaware that he was immoral : and so was Milton in *Paradise Lost* : and so also and for that very reason were the majority of their readers. Happily most of us when we read a book that makes for righteousness are like children reading Shakspeare, who simply do not notice the things that make their elders nervous. It is not that we refuse the evil and choose the good : we are quite unaware of the presence of the evil at all. No doubt that sometimes makes its influence the more powerful because unperceived : and for this kind of subtle influence both Milton and the Old Testament have to answer. But with many happy natures an escape is made by the process of selection : and, as they manage to acquire the God-fearing righteousness of the Old Testament without its ferocity, so they manage to receive from Milton his high emotional consciousness of life as the glad and

free service of God and to ignore altogether
his intellectual description of it as a very one-
sided bargain with a very dangerous Potentate.

Nor must Milton be made, as he often is,
to bear more blame in this matter than he
deserves. Divine tyranny with hell as its
sanction was no invention of his. The
Catholic Church, as all her art shows, had
always made full use of it. And the new
horror of his own day, the Calvinist predestina-
tion, he expressly and frequently repudiates.
The free will of man is the very base of his
system. In it men may suffer, as it seems to
us, out of all proportion to their guilt; but at
least they suffer only for deeds done of their
own free will.

But the true answer to the charge of
corrupting English religious thought so often
brought against Milton is that while the harm
he did must be admitted it was far outweighed
by the good. It could not be for nothing that
generations of readers, as they turned over
Milton's pages, found themselves listening to
the voice of a man to whom God's presence
was the most constant of realities, the most
active of daily and hourly influences : who,
from his youth up, visibly glowed with an
ardent desire for the service of God and man :
who, whatever his faults were, had nothing

base or mean about him, habitually thought
of life as a thing to be lived on the heights,
and by his exalted spirit and unconquerable
will enlarges for those who know him the
whole conception of what a human being may
achieve. It could not be for nothing that on
the topmost heights of English poetry stood
a man who could scarcely finish a single one
of his poems without some soaring ascent
to heaven and heavenly things : whose most
characteristic utterances for himself are such
lines as

" Toward which Time leads me, and the will
    of Heaven " ;

or—

" As ever in my great Task-Master's eye : "

and for others as well as for himself such a
hope as that which concludes his *At a Solemn
Music*—

" O, may we soon again renew that song,
    And keep in tune with Heaven, till God
        ere long
    To his celestial concert us unite,
    To live with Him, and sing in endless morn
        of light ! "

Tu habe Deum prae oculis tuis, says the
author of *The Imitation* : " Have thou God

before Thine eyes." And so by his poetry
and by his life says Milton. The influence of
such a man, whatever the faults of his intellectual creed, can hardly on the whole have been
anything but a good one, either on those who
heard his living voice or on those who for two
hundred years have caught what they may of
it from the printed pages of his books.

So much it seemed worth while to say in
defence of Milton whose sins in these matters
have always been exaggerated by his ecclesiastical and political opponents. But the effect,
good or bad, which a great poem produces on
opinion is a mere by-product : its essential
business is nothing of that sort but the production in the minds of competent readers of
the pleasure proper to a great work of the
imagination. And this is the criterion by
which the *Paradise Lost*, like every other
work of the kind, must primarily be judged.

The poem, as we have it, is the long delayed
result of an intention formed in Milton's
strangely ripe and resolute youth. Before
he was thirty he spoke openly to his friends of
writing a great poem which was, as he shortly
afterwards had no hesitation in telling the
public, to be of the sort that the world does
not willingly let die. At first the subject was
to have been the Arthurian legend which

poets of all ages have found so fruitful. But
that was soon abandoned, apparently for the
reason that a little examination of the authorities convinced the poet that it was not histori-
cally true. This fact has a literary as well as
a biographical importance. Great artist as
Milton was, he seems to have confused truth
of art with truth of fact. He preferred a
Biblical subject because it was his belief that
every statement in the Bible was literally
true. This belief, except from the emotional
fervour it inspired in him, was a positive
disadvantage to him as a poet. It circum-
scribed his freedom of invention, it compelled
him to argue that the action of his drama
as he found it was already reasonable and
probable instead of letting his imagination
work upon it and make it so; it made him aim
too often at producing belief instead of delight
in his hearers. This, of course, had obvious
drawbacks as soon as people ceased to regard
the first chapters of Genesis as a literal prose
record of events which actually happened.
For a hundred and fifty years many people
read the *Paradise Lost* and supposed themselves to be enjoying the poem when what they
were really enjoying was simply the pleasure
of reading their own beliefs expressed in
magnificent verse. In the same way many

religious people imagine that they enjoy early Italian art when they in fact enjoy nothing but its religious sentiment. But neither art nor poetry can live permanently on these extraneous supports. So when less interest came to be felt in Adam and Eve there were fewer readers for *Paradise Lost.* But the readers who were lost were not those that matter For it is a complete mistake to say, as is sometimes said, that the fact that the story of *Paradise Lost* was once believed and now is so no longer is fatal to the interest of the poem. That is not so for the right reader: or at least, so far as it is so, it is Milton's fault and not that of his subject. The *Æneid* loses no more by our disbelief in the historical reality of Æneas or Dido than *Othello* loses by our ignorance whether such a person ever existed. The difficulty, so far as there is one, is not that many readers disbelieve the story of Milton's poem: it is that he himself passionately believed it. If he had been content with offering us his poem as an imaginative creation, if he had not again and again insisted on its historical truth and theological importance, no changes in the views of his readers, no merely intellectual or historical criticism, could have touched him more than they can Virgil. As a poet he is

perfectly invulnerable by any such attacks :
it is only so far as he deserted poetry for
the pseudo-scientific matter-of-fact world of
prose that he fails and irritates us. All the
poetry of *Paradise Lost* is as true to-day as
when it was first written : it is only the
science and logic and philosophy, in a word
the prose, which has proved liable to decay.
There is always that difference between the
works of the imagination and those of
the intellect. A hundred theories about the
Greek legends of the Centaurs or the Amazons
may establish themselves, have a vogue,
undergo criticism and finally be exploded
as absurdities : that is the common fate of
intellectual products after they have done
their work. But the Centaurs of the Parthenon and the Amazons of the Mausoleum
are immortally independent of all changes of
opinion.

This is the first disadvantage of the subject
chosen by Milton, that he believed in it too
much. The fact that he did so and thought
its prose truth all-important at once limited
the freedom of his imagination and diverted
him from the single-minded pursuit of the
proper end of poetry. He was evidently
quite unaware of this drawback and it has
been little, if at all, noticed by his critics.

On the other hand, he was perfectly aware
of what would appear to other people to be
the disadvantages involved in the choice of
a subject so unlike those of previous epics. He
speaks more than once of the novelty of this
theme, the best-known allusion being the
beautiful introduction to Book IX., in which
he describes his subject, that of the human sin
and the divine anger

" That brought into this World a world of
 woe,
Sin and her shadow Death, and Misery,
Death's harbinger : "

and contrasts it with those other sins and
other angers on which Homer and Virgil
built their poems. But he is not afraid of
the contrast : he thinks it is all to his own
advantage—

    " Sad task ! yet argument
Not less but more heroic than the wrath
Of stern Achilles on his foe pursued
Thrice fugitive about Troy wall; or rage
Of Turnus for Lavinia disespoused ;
Or Neptune's ire or Juno's, that so long
Perplexed the Greek, and Cytherea's son :
If answerable style I can obtain
Of my celestial Patroness who deigns
Her nightly visitation unimplored,
And dictates to me slumbering, or inspires
Easy my unpremeditated verse,

Since first this subject for heroic song
Pleased me, long choosing and beginning
    late,
Not sedulous by nature to indite
Wars, hitherto the only argument
Heroic deemed—"

The whole passage is too long for quotation.
Indeed, as we have already had occasion to
notice, it is one of the difficulties of discussing
Milton that quotation is almost always compelled to do him an injury by giving less than
the whole of any one of those long-sustained
flights of music in which he rises and falls,
turns to the left hand or the right, as his
imagination leads him, but always on un-
flagging wings of undoubted and easy security.
But enough has been quoted here to illustrate
the poet's direct challenge of Homer and Virgil
in this matter of subject. He was perfectly
well aware that he was making an entirely
new departure, not only from the subject of
the ancients but also, as is shown by his
detailed condemnation of " tilting furniture,
emblazoned shields " and the rest, from those
of such poets as Ariosto, Tasso and Spenser.
He did it deliberately, with open eyes.   And
there is no doubt that he was at least partly
right.   To this day he and Dante, in their
different ways, enjoy a common advantage

over Homer, and still more over a poet mainly
of fancy like Tasso, in the fact that their
subject, that of the meaning and destiny of
human life, is one in itself of profound and
absorbing interest to all thinking men and
women. Even if their treatment of it be in
some parts and for some people unsatisfying
or irritating they at least have started with
that advantage. A dangerous advantage because, as we have seen in Milton's case and
might also see in Dante's, tempting them to
go outside the pure business of their art;
but still in itself an advantage. Milton was
probably also right in feeling that the fighting
element in the old poets had been greatly
overdone. The most interesting parts of the
Iliad for us to-day are not battles, but such
things as the parting of Hector and Andro-
mache and the scene between Priam and
Achilles. Where the fighting still moves us, as
in the case of Hector and Achilles, or Virgil's
Turnus and Pallas, it is mainly for the sake
of an accompanying human and moral interest
altogether above its own. The miscellaneous
details of weapons and wounds which evidently
once gave so much pleasure are now equally
tedious to us whether it is Homer or Malory
or Morris who narrates them. They can no
longer give interest : they can only receive it

from such intrinsic interest as may belong to
the combatants.

So far Milton had some justification for
preferring his own subject to those of Homer
and Virgil. But, so far as we can judge, he
was entirely unconscious of its disadvantages :
as well of those which it shares with the *Iliad*
and *Æneid* as of those peculiar to itself. Of
the former, the most conspicuous is that
inevitably involved in the introduction of
divine persons into the action. Everybody
feels that Homer's gods constantly spoil the
interest and probability of his story, while
very rarely enhancing its dignity. One never
understands why they can do so much, and
yet do no more, to affect the action. Their
interference is always irritating, generally
immoral, and on the whole ineffective. Their
omnipotence is occasional and irrational : they
are limited in the use of it by each other,
and all alike, even Zeus, are limited by a
shadowy Law or Fate in the background.
Their interventions only make the struggle
seem unfair or unreal, and we are glad to be
rid of them.

Milton is still more deeply involved in the
same difficulty. All his personages except
two are superhuman. It is his great disadvantage as compared with Dante that the

main lines of his story are all scriptural and therefore outside the influence of his invention, that his actors are divine, angelic, or sinless beings, and therefore such as can provide little of the uncertainty of issue or variety of temper and experience which are the stuff of drama. He is hampered by having constantly to assert the true free will and responsibility of Satan for his rebellion and of Adam for his disobedience, even to the extent of putting argumentative soliloquies confessing it into their own mouths. So far he succeeds : both are felt to be free in their fatal choice. But the war in heaven can arouse no interest because its issue is obviously foregone, and much of the action of the rebel angels necessarily conflicts with the frequent statements that they can do nothing except as permitted by their Conqueror. At one moment they know their powerlessness, at another they hope for revenge and victory. These are grave difficulties which deprive large parts of the poem of that illusion of probability or truth without which poetry cannot do its proper work. A further difficulty, from which ancient poets were free, arises from the purely intellectual and spiritual nature of the Christian God. It is as if Homer had had to deal with the divine unity of Plato instead of

with his family of loving, quarrelling, fighting
gods and goddesses. A being who is Incomprehensible as well as Almighty and Omnis-
cient can hardly be an actor in a poem written
for human readers. The gods in the *Iliad*
shock us because they are too like ourselves :
Milton's God may sometimes shock us too :
but He is more often in danger of fatiguing
us by His utter remoteness from our experience,
by His dwelling not merely, not indeed so
often as we could wish, in clouds and darkness,
but in a world of theological mysteries which
necessarily lose more in sublimity than they
gain in clearness by being perpetually discussed and explained. Dante's poem is at
least as full as Milton's of obscure theological
doctrines and attempts at their explanation;
but, either by virtue of the plan of the *Divina
Commedia* or by some finer instinct of reserve
and reverence in the poet, we never find ourselves in Dante as we do in Milton exercising
our critical faculties, whether we will or no, on
the very words of God Himself. If we reject
an argument as unconvincing or fallacious, it
is on Virgil or Statius, Beatrice or Thomas
Aquinas, that we sit in judgment. The Divine
Mind, intensely and constantly felt as its
presence is from the first canto of the poem to
the last, is yet felt always as from behind a

curtain which can never be raised for the sight
of mortal eyes.

Still, it must be admitted that, impossible
as was the task of making the Infinite and
Eternal an actor and speaker in a human poem,
Milton's very failure in it is sublime. His
prodigious powers are nowhere more wonder-
fully displayed than in trying to do what no
one, not even himself, could do. The second
half of his third book, for instance, is far
more interesting than the first, but it may
well be doubted whether the mere fact of his
accomplishing the first at all is not a greater
proof of his poetic genius. Nowhere does
that unfailing certainty of style, in which he
has scarcely an equal among the poets of the
whole world, stand him in such astonishing
stead as in these difficult dialogues in heaven.

" Father, thy word is passed, Man shall find
    grace;
  And shall Grace not find means, that finds
    her way,
  The speediest of thy wingèd messengers.
  To visit all thy creatures, and to all
  Comes unprevented, unimplored, unsought?
  Happy for Man, so coming; "

On the side of invention there is nothing
remarkable; but, on the side of art, what a

divine graciousness there is in its tone and manner; what incomparable skill in the management of the verse! Note the quiet monosyllabic beginning, taking note, as it were, of the decree of mercy, and then the expansion of it, the loving voice pressing forward in freer movement as it confidently proclaims the happy results that cannot fail to follow. And observe the peculiarly Miltonic inter-lacing of the whole, line leading to line and word to word : the "grace" of the first line giving the key to the "grace" of the second, the repeated "find" of the second line and the repeated "all" of the fourth, the "comes" of the fifth line leading on to the "coming" of the sixth. To make a list of such details as these is not to explain the effect which they produce; that is the secret of Milton's genius. So is that cunning variety in the rhythm of the verses : three pauses in the first line, two in the second, only one in the third : the principal pause after the sixth syllable in both the first two lines, and yet the words and their accents so artfully varied that not the slightest monotony is felt; the suggestion of easy flight in the smooth unbroken movement of the third line—

"The speediest of thy wingèd messengers."

Milton knew that an utterance of this kind,
in which the Bible had anticipated him a
hundred times, admitted of no novelty in
itself : and his reverence forbade him to give
his invention free rein in these high matters.
But what he could do he did. The matter
of the speech he leaves as he found it; what
the Son says every reader has heard before :
but after this manner he has not heard it.
In passing through Milton's hands all has been
transformed into a new birth by the consummate craftsmanship of a supreme artist.

Thus the poet escapes, as far as it was
possible to escape, from the difficulties created
for him by his acceptance of divine Persons
as actors in his drama. But the escape could
only be partial. It is true that as Johnson
says, " whatever be done the poet is always
great " : but greatness of style often struggles
in vain against the incongruity of a verbose
and argumentative Deity. Such gods as
Virgil's Venus and Juno may hurl rhetorical
speeches at each other without much ill
effect, but we feel that it was a lack of the
sense of mystery in Milton that kept him
from realizing that the one God, Creator,
Father and Judge of all, cannot with fitness
debate or argue : He can only decree. " Let
thy words be few "; that is even truer, we

instinctively feel, of words put into His mouth than of words addressed to Him. Milton's God suffers even more than Shakspeare's Ghosts from a garrulity which destroys the sense of the awe properly belonging to a supernatural being; and the grim laughter of the Miltonic heaven is in its different way even more fatal to that awe than the Jack-in-the-box appearances and disappearances of the dead Hamlet and Banquo.

Such are some of the difficulties, in part overcome by the poet and in part unperceived, inherent in the subject of *Paradise Lost.* One more, the greatest of all, remains. Poetry is a human art and its subject is human life. In the story Milton set himself to tell there are only two human figures; and how can they, living as they do in isolated perfection and sinlessness, without children or friends, without learning or art or business, without hopes or fears or memories, without the experience of disease or the expectation of death, and therefore without the joy, as we know it, of life and health, how can they provide material for a poem that can interest beings so utterly unlike them as ourselves? The answer is twofold. It is partly that they do fail to provide that material. The *Paradise Lost* has in fact far less of ordinary human life in

F

it, far less variety of action, than the *Iliad*
and *Odyssey*. This was probably unavoidable
but it was probably also Milton's deliberate
intention. It was not his nature to care much
about the small doings of ordinary people in
everyday life. The line which he most often
repeats in *Paradise Lost* is the very opposite
of those which are repeated so often in the
Iliad, verses of no noticeable poetic quality,
just doing their plain duty of linking two
speeches or two paragraphs together : such
as—

ὣς οἱ μὲν τοιαῦτα πρὸς ἀλλήλους ἀγόρευον.

What Milton chooses for repetition is, on the
other hand, one of his stateliest lines, the
magnificent—

" Thrones, Dominations, Princedoms, Virtues,
    Powers."

The choice is characteristic of the man. His
" natural port," as Johnson well said, " is
gigantic loftiness," and his end to " raise the
thoughts above sublunary cares or pleasures."
So it may well be that this disadvantage
of his subject did not weigh with him as
much as it would have done with most poets.
But he was not altogether blind to it, and
the amazing skill he shows in partly getting
over it is the other half of the answer to

the question asked just now. His action up
to the moment of the Fall is the inhuman
one of a few days in hell, heaven, and a
small sinless spot of earth : and the Fall does
not increase the number of actors. Yet into
the mouths of this tiny group of persons
Milton may be said to have brought all the
history of the world and all its geography,
art, science and learning, the Jew, the Christian and the Pagan, Greek philosophy and
Roman politics, classical myth, mediæval
romance, and even the contemporary life of
his own experience. This is partly done, as
Virgil had done it, by the way of a prophecy
of future ages : but to a much greater extent
by the way of similes which are more elaborate
and learned in Milton than in any poet. By
their assistance he gives rest to the imagination
exhausted by the sublimity of heaven and hell,
bringing it home to its own familiar earth,
to scenes whose charm, unlike that of Eden
or Pandemonium, lies not in the wonder their
strangeness excites but in the old habits, experiences and memories which they recall. So,
after the strain of the great debate with which
the second book opens, he soothes us with the
beautiful simile of the evening after storm—

" Thus they their doubtful consultations dark
    Ended, rejoicing in their matchless Chief;

As, when from mountain-tops the dusky
  clouds
Ascending, while the North-wind sleeps,
  o'erspread
Heaven's cheerful face, the louring ele-
  ment
Scowls o'er the darkened landskip snow
  or shower,
If chance the radiant sun, with farewell
  sweet,
Extend his evening beam, the fields revive,
The birds their notes renew, and bleating
  herds
Attest their joy, that hill and valley rings."

Note how large and general it is. Its
method is the classical appeal to universal
knowledge and feeling, not the romantic
method of strangeness of sentiment and
detailed particularity of truth. Matthew
Arnold once recommended those who cannot
read Greek or Latin to read Milton as a far
better key than any translation can be to the
secret of the greatness of the ancient poets.
This is the truth : and not only for the reason
on which Arnold laid just stress—the " sure
and flawless perfection of rhythm and diction "
in which, as he truly says, Milton is unique
among English poets : but also for his classical habit of mind, for his central sanity, for
the sureness with which he makes his call on
the thoughts and emotions, not of eccentric

or exceptional individuals, but of the men and women of all times and all nations.

Yet he can use his similes, as we said, to introduce the life of his own day and still generally carry his classical manner with him. So in the following simile he begins with the Homeric wolf and ends with the Roman and Laudian clergy. Satan has leapt over the wall of Paradise : and the simile begins—

> " As when a prowling wolf,
> Whom hunger drives to seek new haunt for prey,
> Watching where shepherds pen their flocks at eve
> In hurdled cotes amid the field secure,
> Leaps o'er the fence with ease into the fold :
> Or as a thief bent to unhoard the cash
> Of some rich burgher, whose substantial doors,
> Cross-barred and bolted fast, fear no assault,
> In at the window climbs, or o'er the tiles :
> So clomb this first grand Thief into God's fold:
> So since into his Church lewd hirelings climb."

The last line smacks perhaps more of the angry pamphleteer than fits with classical sanity : but how admirably the London citizen's house gives vivid reality to the beautiful remoteness of the wolf which English shepherds had long forgotten to fear; how the recollection, present to every reader's

mind, of that very same simile in the Gospel
of St. John, prepares the way for its religious
application here : how the attention is seized
by that magnificent line of arresting monosyllables, each heavy with the sense of fate—

" So clomb this first grand Thief into God's
    fold ! "

It used to be said that Milton uses monosyllables to express slowness of action. But
that is notably not the case here. And in
the main it seems that he uses them, as
Shakspeare often did, for expressing the
solemnity of grave crisis, or for deep emotion,
when anything fanciful, ornate or verbose
would be fatal to the simplicity, akin to
silence, which all men find fitting at great
moments. So Shakspeare makes Kent say at
Lear's death—

" Vex not his ghost ; O let him pass ! he hates
    him
  That would upon the rack of this tough
    world
  Stretch him out longer."

And so Milton uses these tremendous monosyllables, like a bell tolling into the silence of
midnight, to force our attention on the doom
of all the world that took its beginning when
Satan entered Paradise—

" So clomb this first grand Thief into God's
    fold."

So again, with less solemnity as befitting a
less awful person but still with arresting and
delaying emphasis, he records the actual
eating of the fatal apple—

                        " she plucked, she eat :
Earth felt the wound, and Nature from her
    seat,
Sighing through all her works, gave signs of
    woe.
That all was lost."

So he suspends the flow of the richest and
most elaborate of his similes by the slow-
moving monosyllables of

            " which cost Ceres all that pain
    To seek her through the world : "

So he strikes the deepest note, beyond all
politics, of his debate in hell :

" And that must end us; that must be our
    cure—
    To be no more : "

So again he closes the first Act of *Paradise
Regained* with a verse of solitary awe—

" And now wild beasts come forth the woods
    to roam."

But to return to the similes. Milton uses them, as we have seen, to introduce things familiar and contemporary into the remote and majestic theme of his poem. But he also uses them to introduce the whole world into Eden, all later history into the beginning of the world, all the varied glories of art and war, poetry and legend, with which his memory was stored, into an action which was only partly human and provided no scope at all for any human activities except of the most primitive order. So the palace of Hell is, he tells us, something far beyond the magnificence of " Babylon, or great Alcairo "; and the army of rebel angels far exceeds those

" That fought at Thebes and Ilium, on each
      side
    Mixed with auxiliar gods; and what re-
      sounds
    In fable or romance of Uther's son,
    Begirt with British and Armoric knights;
    And all who since, baptized or infidel,
    Jousted in Aspramont or Montalban,
    Damasco, or Marocco, or Trebisond,
    Or whom Biserta sent from Afric shore,
    When Charlemain with all his peerage fell
    By Fontarabbia."

So, in another of his returns to those tales and fancies of the Middle Age which, in spite of his intellectual and moral rejection of their falsity, yet always moved him to unusual beauty of verse, he compares the dwarfed rebels of Hell to the

> "faery elves,
> Whose midnight revels, by a forest side
> Or fountain, some belated peasant sees,
> Or dreams he sees, while overhead the Moon
> Sits arbitress, and nearer to the Earth
> Wheels her pale course; they, on their mirth and dance
> Intent, with jocund music charm his ear;
> At once with joy and fear his heart rebounds."

So Eve at her gardening recalls Pales, or Pomona or

> " Ceres in her prime,
> Yet virgin of Proserpina from Jove."

And so, in an earlier book, the beauty of Paradise itself, too great to be directly told, is, like the splendour of Pandemonium, conveyed to us by the most perfect of those negative similes which, forced upon Milton by the narrow bounds of his story, are perhaps the most distinctive of all the glories of *Paradise Lost*. It is too long to quote in full : but a few lines may be given : and they must include the first four, one of which has just

F 2

been quoted, verses of such amazing beauty
that, if Milton could be represented by four
lines, these might well be the chosen four—

> "Not that fair field
> Of Enna, where Proserpin gathering flowers,
> Herself a fairer flower, by gloomy Dis
> Was gathered, which cost Ceres all that pain
> To seek her through the world; nor that sweet
>   grove
> Of Daphne by Orontes, and the inspired
> Castalian spring, might with this Paradise
> Of Eden strive."

But it is time to leave Milton's similes,
though similes play a more important part in
Paradise Lost than in any other epic. Indeed their necessary absence is a great element
in the comparative dulness of the books given
over to the discourses of Raphael and Michael.
A single chapter in a little book of this kind
can only deal with one or two aspects of so
great a subject as *Paradise Lost*. That being
so, it is best, perhaps, to touch on points in
which Milton stands pre-eminent or unique.
The similes are one of these. Another is the
splendour of the Miltonic speeches. It is one
of the defects of *Paradise Lost* that its actors
are seldom soldiers whom all the ages agree
to admire, and often theologians whom all
fear or dislike, or politicians whom all obey

and despise. Yet how magnificently Milton turns this weakness into a strength! His speeches have not the eternal humanity of Homer's : but as oratory, above all as debating oratory, they have no poetic rivals outside the drama. The poet who had lived through the Long Parliament and the trial of Strafford knew the art of speech as Homer could not know it. It may seem strange to us that the political struggle of his day affected him so much more than the military; but the fact is so. Pym and Hampden are felt in *Paradise Lost* far more than Fairfax or Cromwell. The speeches of the second book could only have been written by the citizen of a free state who had lived through a crisis in its fortunes. Other speeches in the poem—that incomparable one of Eve to Adam in the fourth book, " Sweet is the breath of morn," those that pass between Eve and Adam after the Fall and Adam's Job-like lament in the tenth book—have a purer human beauty about them : but of the oratory of debate no poem in the world provides a more magnificent display than the second book of *Paradise Lost*. The debate is a real debate. The opening of Moloch, " My sentence is for open war," would be instantly effective in any Parliament in the world. It rouses attention by its directness, it compels adherence as only courage can. To undo its effect Belial has to employ the most subtle of all oratorical arts, that of accepting the arguments which he dare not directly combat and then gradually turning them to the confusion of their author. So he and Mammon bring the assembly completely round to the mood of ease and acquiescence. Then follows the tremendous figure of Beelzebub, an aged Chatham or Gladstone, who

> " in his rising seemed
> A pillar of state.   Deep on his front engraven
> Deliberation sat and public care;
> And princely counsel in his face yet shone,
> Majestic though in ruin.   Sage he stood,
> With Atlantean shoulders fit to bear
> The weight of mightiest monarchies; his look
> Drew audience and attention still as night,
> Or summer's noon-tide air."

Yet Milton's consciousness of the situation as it really would be is such that Beelzebub does not dare to revive Moloch's defeated policy of war. To talk of fighting to cowed rebels who have just been taught the too pleasant lesson of the folly of further resistance would have been useless. So he begins by telling them that the ease promised to them is a delusion : they may submit, but submission

will never win them peace, or deliver them
from their victorious enemy. Peace, then,
they cannot have; and must have war:
but it need not be open or dangerous: craft
has its weapons as well as force: "what if
we find Some easier enterprise" than the
perilous folly of assaulting heaven?

Such a sketch may just serve to show that
the great debate is a living thing in which we
feel the temper of the audience submitting
to the successive orators and in its turn re-
acting upon them. Another proof of the
actuality of Milton's oratory is the way in
which it can be quoted.

" I give not Heaven for lost : "

" Which, if not victory, is yet revenge : "

> " What though the field be lost?
> All is not lost; the unconquerable will,
> And study of revenge, immortal hate,
> And courage never to submit or yield,
> And what is else not to be overcome: "

> " what peace can we return
> But, to our power, hostility and hate?"

> " This would surpass
> Common revenge, and interrupt his joy
> In our confusion : "

> " Advise if this be worth
> Attempting, or to sit in darkness here
> Hatching vain empires: "

> " What reinforcement we may gain from hope,
> If not, what resolution from despair : "

> " on whom we send
> The weight of all and our last hope relies : "

> " This enterprise
> None shall partake with me."

All these have been or could well be hurled
by contending Parliamentarians across the
table of the House of Commons, often with
a fine irony, the Miltonic magnificence em-
phasizing the pettiness of the ordinary political squabbles.   But, of course, the theological
questions which are at the root of Milton's
debate make many of the arguments inap-
plicable to politics : indeed, what is probably
the most remembered passage in all the
speeches has nothing to do with social or
political activities but draws its poignant
interest from the secret thoughts that visit
the hearts of men when they are most alone—

> " And that must end us; that must be our
>   cure,
>   To be no more.   Sad cure ! for who would
>   lose,
>   Though full of pain, this intellectual being,

> Those thoughts that wander through
>   eternity,
> To perish rather, swallowed up and lost
> In the wide womb of uncreated Night,
> Devoid of sense and motion ? "

Here we obviously go outside the dramatic
probabilities : it is no longer Belial who is
speaking : it is the voice of a highly cultivated
and intellectual human being with all Greek
thought behind him; it is, in short, Milton
himself. The whole poem is full of such
autobiographical confessional passages, either
indirect like this or open and undisguised like
the great introductions to the first, third,
seventh and ninth books. This constant
intervention of the poet in his epic is one of
the originalities of *Paradise Lost,* and certainly
not the least successful. The passages which
are due to it have been criticized as irregu-
larities or superfluities, but, as Johnson
justly asked, " superfluities so beautiful who
would take away ? " Homer may be said
never to allow us to do more than guess
obscurely at what he himself was or
thought or felt : so leaving room for the
follies of the criticism which supposes him to
be a kind of limited company of poets. Virgil
spoke directly to his readers at least once
in the *Æneid,* in the most magnificent, and

most magnificently fulfilled, of all the poetic promises of eternal fame—

" Fortunati ambo ! Si quid mea carmina
       possunt
Nulla dies unquam memori vos eximet ævo
Dum domus Æneæ Capitoli immobile
       saxum
Accolet imperiumque pater Romanus habe-
       bit."

But it is less in such a direct intervention as this than in the whole tone and temper of his poem that he reveals to us his delicate and beautiful nature.   Milton confesses himself in both ways.   His high seriousness, his proud and resolute will, his grave sadness at the folly of mankind, are interwoven in the whole of his story.   Then in the speeches he will often, as in this of Belial, forget altogether who is speaking and where and when, forget Satan and Adam, Eden and Hell, and make his human escape to his own time and country and to himself.   The extreme limitations of his subject made something of this kind almost necessary.   When all had been done that simile and prophecy could do to bring in the life of men and women as Milton's readers knew it there still remained the difficulty that Adam and his angel visitors must talk, and that before the Fall there was almost nothing for them to talk about. So they constantly talk as if they had all history behind them and the world's processes were to them, as to us, old and familiar things. " War seemed a civil game To this uproar," says Raphael, as if he were fresh from reading Livy or Gibbon and had all the wars of Europe and Asia in his memory. Often Milton calls attention, as it were, to his own inconsistencies, putting in an apology like that of Michael when he talks to Adam about Hamath and Hermon—

" Things by their names I call though yet
    unnamed ; "

but more often he leaves them unexplained, perhaps not even noticing them himself. These difficulties are seen at their worst in the very earthly geography of heaven and its very unheavenly military operations : and, interesting as the passages are, it is difficult to forget the incongruity of Raphael and Adam discussing the Ptolemaic and Copernican theories of the universe, or Adam moralizing on the unhappiness of marriage as if he had studied the divorce reports or gone through a course of modern novels. Yet few and foolish are the readers who can dwell on dramatic improbabilities when Adam

is pouring out the bitter cry wrung from
Milton by the still unforgotten miseries of his
first marriage—

               " Oh ! why did God,
Creator wise, that peopled highest Heaven
With Spirits masculine, create at last
This novelty on Earth, this fair defect
Of Nature, and not fill the World at once
With men as Angels, without feminine,
Or find some other way to generate
Mankind ?   This mischief had not then be-
    fallen,
And more that shall befall; innumerable
Disturbances on Earth through female snares,
And strait conjunction with this sex. For
    either
He never shall find out fit mate, but such
As some misfortune brings him, or mistake;
Or whom he wishes most shall seldom gain,
Through her perverseness, but shall see her
    gained
By a far worse, or, if she love, withheld
By parents; or his happiest choice too late
Shall meet, already linked and wedlock-
    bound
To a fell adversary, his hate or shame;
Which infinite calamity shall cause
To human life, and household peace con-
    found."

It is obvious that in all this we hear the
poet's own voice. But it is scarcely fair to
quote it without pointing out that it must

not be taken alone. The common notion
that Milton's own melancholy experience had
made him a purblind misogynist is a complete mistake. No one has praised marriage
as he has. The chastest of poets is as little
afraid as the Prayer Book of frank acceptance
of the physical facts which must commonly
be the basis of its spiritual relation. It is
the whole union for which he stands, of body,
mind, and spirit. He puts into the mouth
of this same Adam the most eloquent praise
woman ever received, culminating in

" All higher Knowledge in her presence falls
　Degraded. Wisdom in discourse with her
　Loses discountenanced, and like Folly shows;
　Authority and Reason on her wait,
　As one intended first, not after made
　Occasionally : and, to consummate all,
　Greatness of mind and nobleness their seat
　Build in her loveliest, and create an awe
　About her, as a guard angelic placed."

It is true that the reply of the Angel
moderating these ardours is more evidently
Miltonic—
　　　　　　　" what transports thee so ?
An outside ? fair no doubt and worthy well
Thy cherishing, thy honouring, and thy love;
Not thy subjection. Weigh with her thyself;
Then value. Oft-times nothing profits more
Than self-esteem, grounded on just and right."

But, though in these last words Raphael
entirely disappears in Milton, the poet who
could conceive the panegyric to which Raphael
replies, who could elsewhere make his hero
say that he received " access in every virtue "
from the looks of Eve, had assuredly no low
ideal of what a woman may be. Adam speaks
for him when he praises love as

> " not the lowest end of human life; "

and he gives us a true corrective of the over-
severe picture of Milton which half-knowledge
is apt to draw when he goes on to declare
that

> " not to irksome toil, but to delight,
> He made us, and delight to reason joined."

But this is only one of many subjects on
which Milton lets us hear his own voice speaking through his characters. We hear it when
Satan cries to Beelzebub—

> " Fallen Cherub, to be weak is miserable,
> Doing or suffering : "

when Raphael reports Nisroch as saying of
pain and pleasure what may well have been
felt by the blind poet who owed his knowledge
of pleasure to memory only, while he knew

pain by the frequent experience of one of the
most painful of diseases—

> " sense of pleasure we may well
> Spare out of life, perhaps, and not repine,
> But live content, which is the calmest life;
> But pain is perfect misery, the worst
> Of evils, and, excessive, overturns
> All patience : "

we hear it when Adam, like a weary scholar,
says that

> " not to know at large of things remote
> From use, obscure and subtle, but to know
> That which before us lies in daily life,
> Is the prime wisdom; "

when Raphael asks, like a Platonic philosopher,
> " what if Earth
> Be but the shadow of Heaven, and things
> therein
> Each to other like, more than on Earth is
> thought ? "

when Adam, like a doubting Christian in an
age of speculation, hesitates for a moment
about the efficacy of prayer—

> " that from us aught should ascend to
> Heaven
> So prevalent as to concern the mind
> Of God high-blest, or to incline his will,
> Hard to belief may seem : "

and once more when Adam cries—

" solitude sometimes is best society,"

as if he, like the blind Milton, was worn out
by twenty years of contending voices, and
longed for the relief of silent and lonely
thought.

To the direct interventions of the poet
there is less need to call attention as, of
course, no reader can miss them. They
are probably the most universally admired
passages of the poem. Every reader who
deserves to read them at all finds himself
unable to do so without wishing to get them
by heart. They do not rival the daring
splendour of the scenes in hell : nor perhaps
the suave and gracious perfection of the
evening scene in Paradise in the fourth book;
nor can they, of course, exhibit the dramatic
power of the scene that precedes and still
more of those that follow the Fall. But
nothing in the whole poem moves us so much.
It is not merely that Milton has exerted his
whole mastery of his art to make their every
line and every word please the ear, awaken
the memory, stimulate the imagination, lift
the whole mental and emotional nature of
the reader up to a height of being unknown
to its ordinary experience. This he has

done in some other parts of his poem. But, fine as some of his dramatic touches are, the essence of his genius was rather lyrical than dramatic or objective. And so none of his characters, divine, diabolic or human, will ever move us quite as he moves us himself.

Let us hear the most beautiful of all these confessions : and for once let us indulge ourselves with the whole. The themes that make up Milton's great symphony ought in truth always to be given unbroken, if only that were possible. Indeed, there is a sense in which it may be said that nothing less than the whole poem can do justice to a design so majestic as that of *Paradise Lost*. But in any case it is certain that no fragment of a few lines can convey a full impression of the rhythmical, intellectual, imaginative unity of the Miltonic paragraph or section. This is above all conspicuous in the great speeches and in the elaborate introductions that precede the first, third, seventh and ninth books. Here is the greatest of the four; the most famous of Milton's personal interventions in his poem, and one of the most wonderful things he ever wrote.

" Hail, holy Light, offspring of Heaven first-
    born !
Or of the Eternal coeternal beam

May I express thee unblamed?   Since God
    is light,
And never but in unapproached light
Dwelt from eternity; dwelt then in thee,
Bright effluence of bright essence increate !
Or hearest thou rather pure Ethereal stream,
Whose fountain who shall tell?   Before the
    Sun,
Before the Heavens, thou wert, and at the
    voice
Of God, as with a mantle, didst invest
The rising World of waters dark and deep,
Won from the void and formless Infinite !
Thee I revisit now with bolder wing,
Escaped the Stygian pool, though long
    detained
In that obscure sojourn, while in my flight,
Through utter and through middle Darkness
    borne,
With other notes than to the Orphean
    lyre,
I sung of Chaos and eternal Night,
Taught by the Heavenly Muse to venture
    down
The dark descent, and up to re-ascend,
Though hard and rare: thee I revisit
    safe,
And feel thy sovran vital lamp; but thou
Revisit'st not these eyes, that roll in vain
To find thy piercing ray, and find no
    dawn;
So thick a drop serene hath quenched their
    orbs,
Or dim suffusion veiled.   Yet not the more
Cease I to wander where the Muses haunt

Clear spring, or shady grove, or sunny hill,
Smit with the love of sacred song; but chief
Thee, Sion, and the flowery brooks beneath,
That wash thy hallowed feet, and warbling
    flow,
Nightly I visit; nor sometimes forget
Those other two equalled with me in fate,
So were I equalled with them in renown,
Blind Thamyris and blind Mæonides,
And Tiresias and Phineus, prophets old:
Then feed on thoughts that voluntary move
Harmonious numbers; as the wakeful bird
Sings darkling, and, in shadiest covert hid,
Tunes her nocturnal note. Thus with the
    year
Seasons return; but not to me returns
Day or the sweet approach of even or morn,
Or sight of vernal bloom, or summer's rose,
Or flocks, or herds, or human face divine;
But cloud instead and ever-during dark
Surrounds me, from the cheerful ways of
    men
Cut off, and, for the book of knowledge
    fair,
Presented with a universal blank
Of Nature's works, to me expunged and
    rased,
And wisdom at one entrance quite shut out.
So much the rather thou, Celestial Light,
Shine inward, and the mind through all her
    powers
Irradiate; there plant eyes; all mist from
    thence
Purge and disperse, that I may see and tell
Of things invisible to mortal sight."

Not all the poetry of all the world can produce more than a few passages that equal this
in moving power. Tears are not very far
from the eye that is passing over its page :
tears in which sympathy plays a smaller part
than joy at the discovery that human words
can be so beautiful. But if Milton moves us
more by his own personality than by that of
any of his creations, it is still true that he is
not so entirely without dramatic power as
has sometimes been alleged. No one would
claim for him that he was one of the great
narrative or dramatic masters. But his weakness on these sides is so obvious that there has
been a tendency to exaggerate it. We notice
the undramatic speeches of Satan and Adam :
we notice such things as Eve's dream in the
fifth book which, anticipating, as it does, so
many of the details of her temptation, renders
her fall much less probable, and goes far to
destroy its interest when it occurs. But we
are slower to notice the admirable dramatic
management of such a scene as that between
Eve and the Serpent in the ninth book. And
yet how finely imagined it is, in all its successive stages ! Satan, at first " stupidly
good," overawed at Eve's beauty and innocence; then, recovering his natural malice,
and beginning his attempt by appealing to

two things, curiosity and the love of flattery,
which have always been supposed especially
powerful with women; and Eve, taking no
direct notice of his compliments and in
appearance surrendering only to the other
bait of novelty and surprise; " how cam'st
thou speakable of mute?" So the scene
begins. Flattery has ensured the tempter
a favourable reception; curiosity gives him
the chance of an apparently telling argument.
I ate, he says, of the fruit of a certain tree and
received from it speech and reason. But I
have found nothing to satisfy my new-won
powers till I saw thee, whom I now desire to
worship as the " sovran of creatures." She
affects to rebuke the flattery, but naturally
asks to be shown the tree on which the
wonderful fruit grows. It of course turns out
to be the Forbidden Tree : and Eve mentions
the prohibition as a thing final and un-
questionable. He meets her refusal by giving
a sinister and plausible explanation of the
prohibition. Why did God forbid her the
fruit? " Why, but to keep ye low and
ignorant, His worshippers?" God, he suggests,
knows too well that as the fruit had raised
the serpent from brute to human, so it would
raise the woman from human to divine.
Noon and hunger come to fortify his argu-

ments; and, after a speech in which she adds one more of her own drawn from the name, the Tree of Knowledge, given to the tree by God Himself, she plucks and eats. In the first ecstasy of pleasure she luxuriates in joy and self-confidence. Then she considers whether she shall use her new powers to make herself the equal and even the superior of Adam. The prospect tempts her : but she is not quite free from fear that the threatened punishment of death may after all descend upon her. And that suggests the picture of "Adam wedded to another Eve," which brings her swiftly to the decision that Adam shall share with her her fate, whichever it be, bliss or woe. In this, as later in her hasty proposal of suicide, Eve is a living and convincing human figure. To the stronger and wiser Adam it was harder to give life. But what could be finer or truer than his instant repudiation of her plausible tale—

"How art thou lost ! how on a sudden lost,
    Defaced, deflowered, and now to death
        devote ! "

followed by his immediate resolution to die with her—

"And me with thee hath ruined : for with thee
    Certain my resolution is to die.
    How can I live without thee ? "

The rest follows with equal probability.
Once resolved to unite his lot with hers, he
soon finds arguments to prove that that lot
is not likely after all to be so dreadful. Having
talked himself into the surrender of his judgment he eats, and having eaten he goes at
once all lengths of extravagance, folly and
sin. Then comes the reaction and the inevitable mutual reproaches; with the fine
natural touch of Eve upbraiding Adam for his
weakness in yielding to her request and
granting her the freedom which had proved
so fatal. So the ninth book closes. When
the story is resumed in the second half of the
tenth book we get the tremendous lamenta-
tion of Adam, so strangely undramatic in its
argumentative justification of his own punishment, so full of true drama as well as of
magnificent lyrical power in its cry of human
misery and despair. Then follows the bitter
attack upon Eve, as the cause of all his woe :
and the whole scene is concluded by her
humble and beautiful submission—

" While yet we live, scarce one short hour
        perhaps,
    Between us two let there be peace : "

by their reconciliation, and by their quiet and
resigned acceptance of their common fate.

It was perhaps worth while to go through one act of Milton's drama in this detail to give some idea of the skill which he has shown in working up a few verses of Genesis into an elaborate story. But no detail, no fragmentary notes of any kind, even when they deal with matters in which Milton was far stronger than he was on the side of narrative or drama, can do much to exhibit the greatness of *Paradise Lost.* For that there is only one way, to read it. And, as we said just now, to read the whole. It is true that you cannot read it for the interest of the story as you can all the *Odyssey,* much of the *Iliad* and some of the *Æneid* : but the poem is still a whole and you need the whole to judge and understand it. And even the weaker books, the fifth, the seventh and twelfth, contain episodes, like the scene between Abdiel and Satan and the incomparable conclusion of the whole poem, which are among the last a wise reader would wish to miss. Moreover, where the story is dullest it has things which give, perhaps, the most astonishing proof of Milton's power of style. It is true that he does himself occasionally fall into the empty pomposity which characterized his eighteenth-century imitators who fancied that big words could turn prose into poetry. So he talks of dried fruits as " what by frugal

storing firmness gains To nourish, and superfluous moist consumes." But the thing most
remarkable about this is its extreme rarity.
Taking the poem as a whole, the mighty music
scarcely ceases : the majestic flight of the poet
continues uninterrupted : no contrary winds
disturb it, no weariness brings it flagging
down to earth. There is nothing, not even
theological disputes, out of which he cannot
make fine verse, and occasionally great
poetry. There is nothing, however great,
that he cannot make his own. Just as
Shakspeare took the noble prose of North's
Plutarch, and hardly altering a word made
noble poetry of it, so Milton can take the
Bible. " For now," says Job, " I should
have lain still and been quiet, I should have
slept : then had I been at rest." North could
not rise to the height of this. But even this
Milton will dare to lay his hand upon : and,
if even he cannot lift it any higher, only he
could have touched it at all without desecra-
tion. " How glad," says Adam—

" how glad would lay me down
As in my mother's lap ! There I should rest,
And sleep secure."

Or take a passage like that of the Son of God
clothing Adam and Eve after the Fall, where

many Biblical suggestions are gathered together—

" As when he washed his servants' feet, so
    now
As father of his family he clad
Their nakedness with skins of beasts, or
    slain,
Or, as the snake, with youthful coat repaid;
And thought not much to clothe his
    enemies."

The full appreciation of a passage like this,
so very simple, so apparently obvious, yet so
entirely in the grand style which, whether
his subject stoops or soars, very rarely fails
Milton, is not a thing of one reading or of two.
Milton, the greatest artist of our language,
is naturally the most conspicuous instance
of the law which applies to all great art.
Only natures as rarely endowed with the
receptive gift as he was himself with the
creative can fully appreciate his work at
the first reading. Like all great works of the
imagination it has generally to train, sometimes almost to create, the faculties which
are to appreciate it aright. This is particularly true in the case of classical art, where
the emotional appeal, though just as real, is
much less apparent because it is so much
more controlled by intellectual sanity. Gothic

and Romantic art are commonly far more
instantaneous in the impression they make,
perhaps because, according to the ingenious
suggestion of the Poet Laureate, they admit
at once of more daring flights of the imagination and of stronger realism than classical
art can bear. But it may well be doubted
whether the wonder and delight which every
man of the most modest æsthetic capacity
owes to them can in the end keep pace with
the slower growing appreciation of the universality and sanity of classical work. But
this is an old dispute not likely to be settled
this year or next. Nor does it affect the fact
that all great work, even Romantic or Gothic,
gains by time in proportion to its greatness.
It is the only absolutely certain test of greatness in art. The instantly popular tune is
unendurable in six months, the instantly
popular novel or poem is totally forgotten
in a year or two. No one perceives the whole
greatness of St. Paul's Cathedral, or Sansovino's Library at Venice, or the music of Bach,
or the poetry of Milton, at the first sight or
hearing. No competent eye, ear or mind
fails to perceive more and more of it at each
renewed experience. Whatever be the art,
a picture, a piece of sculpture, a book, the
test is the same : the cheap, the sentimental,

G

the sensational, the merely pretty, lose something, be it little or much, at each renewal of
acquaintance : the great work steadily gains.
To this test *Paradise Lost* can fearlessly
appeal.   It is not meant for idle hours or
empty people.   It is not amusing in the lower
sense of the word.   It is not as exciting as it
might well have been.   It is probably true
that, as Johnson said with his usual honesty,
" No one ever wished it longer than it is " :
yet there is equal truth in another remark of
his, " I cannot wish Milton's work other than
it is," and in the implied answer to his bold
question, " What other author ever soared so
high or sustained his flight so long? "   The
difficulty for Milton's readers is that they do
not easily soar, and still less easily sustain
their soaring.   The great gifts which Johnson
brought to the criticism of literature lay far
more in common sense and in a profound
insight into human life than in any real turn
for poetry.   Of that nearly every one who
to-day gives much time to reading poetry will
probably have as much as he.   Such people
are sometimes mistakenly content with a single
reading of *Paradise Lost*.   They remember
a few of its glories and the rest of the
poem they acquiesce in forgetting.   Let them
put it to the test to which lovers of music

put the Symphonies of Beethoven and lovers
of sculpture the remains of the Parthenon
and the temple of the Ephesian Artemis.
Let them give the little time required to read
it through every year, or every second year.
They will find more in it the second time than
they did the first, and much more the fifth or
the tenth time.   It will issue triumphantly
from the trial : and before they reach middle
age they will know by their own personal
experience, what the best authorities have
always told them, that this is one of those
rare works of human genius whose power
and beauty may in sober truth be called
inexhaustible.

CHAPTER V

PARADISE REGAINED, like the *Odyssey*, the *Æneid* and the second part of *Faust*, has been an inevitable victim of the human taste for comparison. It cannot fail to be compared with *Paradise Lost* and cannot fail to suffer by it. The poets and critics have indeed been kinder to it than the public. Johnson said that if it had not been written by Milton " it would receive universal praise." Wordsworth thought it " the most perfect in execution of anything written by Milton." But the great body of readers finds an epic with only two main actors in it, and hardly anything that can be called a story, too severe a demand upon its poetic taste. And when unprofessional opinion remains constant for several generations, as it has in this case, it is never wise to ignore or defy it. *Paradise Regained* is a very bare poem. It has none of the splendours of its predecessor : no

196

scenes in which we hear the full voice of
that Milton

" Whose Titan angels, Gabriel, Abdiel,
  Starr'd from Jehovah's gorgeous armouries,
  Tower, as the deep-domed empyrean
  Rings to the roar of an angel onset; "

nor yet any of those others which delighted
Tennyson even more, the scenes of Adam's

" bowery loneliness,
The brooks of Eden mazily murmuring,
And bloom profuse and cedar arches."

It has no love, no sin, no quarrel, no
reconciliation, no central moment of tragic
suspense, indeed no human action at all. And
Milton has refrained almost absolutely from
adorning it with the similes which are among
the chief glories of *Paradise Lost*. It is, in
fact, as Mark Pattison has said, " probably
the most unadorned poem extant in any
language."

At the very beginning of *Paradise Lost*
Milton had cast his eye on to that second
chapter in the Christian history of man without which the first is a mere picture of despair.
His subject was to be man's first disobedience
and its results; death, woe and loss of Eden

" till one greater Man
Restore us and regain the blissful seat."

Whether he then had any thought of
attempting to deal with that restoration we
do not know.   Nor do we know what motives
induced him to choose the story of the
Temptation in the Wilderness as the action
in which the new order of things was to be
manifested.   Some critics have been surprised that he did not take the Crucifixion or
the Resurrection.   And it is obvious that the
first, with the Tree of Calvary pointing back
to the Tree in the Garden, would have afforded
a natural sequence to *Paradise Lost.*   Others
have wondered that he did not use the
Descent into Hell in which the liberation of
Satan's captives would have followed on the
story of how they fell into his power.   And
it is obvious that there were great poetic, and
especially Miltonic, possibilities in the theme
of the victorious Son of God entering the
very kingdom in which the Satan of *Paradise
Lost* had exercised such splendid rule, and
setting free the saints and prophets and kings
of the Old Testament.   But it is possible, as
Sir Walter Raleigh has suggested, that Milton
was no longer in the vein for grandiose themes
of external majesty and might such as this
story would have afforded.   " His interest
was now centred rather in the sayings of the
wise than in the deeds of the mighty."   That

may be so : though his *Samson* which was yet to come is certainly not without its mighty deeds. But, whatever were his reasons for putting aside such subjects as the Descent into Hell, it is not difficult to discover several which he probably found decisive in inducing him to prefer the Temptation to the Passion. To begin with, he must have been conscious of the immensely greater difficulty of handling the story of the Passion in such a way that Christian readers could bear to read it. Then, even more certainly operative on his mind was the fact that the Passion is related to us in great detail, the Temptation in a few words of mysterious import; so that the one leaves almost no freedom of invention to the poet, while the other scarcely binds him at all. Then again there is the close parallelism between the temptation in the Garden and the temptation in the Wilderness; and finally, most important of all, the fact that the Temptation is the only event in the life of Christ in which Satan plays a visible and important part. A poem that was to be a second part of *Paradise Lost* could not do without Satan; and in fact he is even more prominent in *Paradise Regained*, where he is present throughout, than in its predecessor of which there are several books which scarcely so

much as mention him. This was no doubt
decisive.

So Milton chose the Temptation in the
Wilderness as his subject, with Satan once
more as one of the two principal actors in
his story. But the actor is even more changed
than the story. The Satan of the later poem
is no longer the splendid rebel of *Paradise
Lost*. *Paradise Regained* has in it no heavenly
battles and its council of devils is a mere
shadow of the great parliament of hell. It
has, therefore, no place either for the general
of the infernal armies or for the Prime Minister
of the infernal Senate. The magnificent figure
who imposes himself on the imagination—

" Like Teneriffe or Atlas unremoved "—

becomes in it something far less impressive,
a political theorist instead of a statesman, a
student of the balance of power instead of a
soldier, a casuistical disputant about culture
and morals in place of a devil venturing all
for empire and revenge. It is as if Alexander
were exchanged for Aristotle : almost as if
St. George were replaced by Mr. Worldly
Wiseman. The imagination is affected by
the inevitable loss of colour, and *Paradise
Regained* is the sufferer in fame and popularity.

It also suffers from the old difficulty inherent in supernatural personages which affects it even more than *Paradise Lost.* The whole action is a succession of Tempta tions. The question how far such attempts by a devil upon a Divine Being can afford any hope to the one or any fear or danger to the other is a mystery of which the Church itself scarcely claims to offer a full explana- tion. Into the theological difficulty this is not the place to enter. It is only with the corresponding poetic difficulty that we are concerned. Just as in *Paradise Lost* it is impossible not to feel the unreality of the war in heaven, so in *Paradise Regained* it is impossible not to feel, in spite of some incon- sistency of language on the subject, that Satan commonly knows who it is whom he is assailing and is known by Him in return, and that consequently the whole action has for poetic purposes a certain unreality. He knows that Jesus is the Son of God; with a right to the homage of all nature and the power to take all as His own. He asks—

" Hast thou not right to all created things ?
Owe not all creatures, by just right, to thee
Service and duty ? "

Yet he discusses with Him various very human methods of arriving at power, just as

G 2

if He were subject to the same conditions as other men who desire to rule or influence the world. The consequence is that, although the speeches contain much interesting thought and much fine poetry, they are seldom or never dramatically convincing. Our Lord, in particular, instead of the gracious and winning figure of the Gospels, becomes a kind of self-sufficient aristocratic moralist. His speeches, as Milton gives them, display rather the defiant virtue of the Stoic, or the self-conscious righteousness of the Pharisee, than the simple and loving charity of the Christian. The weapon of moral and intellectual contempt, so freely employed in them and so natural both to Jew and to Greek, strikes to us a false and jarring note when put into the mouth of Him who taught His disciples that the only way of entry into His kingdom was that of being born again and becoming as little children.

These are all serious drawbacks and they are not the only ones. If from one point of view Milton in *Paradise Regained* is too little of a Christian, from another he is too much. One of the gravest difficulties with which Christian apologists have always had to contend is the entire indifference of the New Testament and, generally speaking, of the

Church in all ages, especially the most devout, not only to economic and material progress, but to all elements except the ethical and spiritual in the higher civilization of humanity. At its friendliest the Church has hardly ever been willing to allow to such things any inherent or independent importance of their own. Those who feel that they owe an incalculable debt to art and poetry and philosophy and therefore to the Greeks, have inevitably found this attitude a stumbling-block. And they will always read with exceptional surprise and indignation the narrow obscurantism of the speech which Milton, scholar and artist as he was, is not ashamed to put into the mouth of Christ in the fourth book. He cannot himself have been a victim of the shallow fallacy expressed in line 325 (he who reads gets little benefit unless he brings judgment to his reading "and what he brings what need he elsewhere seek?"); and his lifelong practice shows that he did not think Greek poetry was

" Thin-sown with aught of profit or delight."

Nor could he have seriously thought that the Hebrew prophets taught "the solid rules of civil government," of which in fact they knew nothing except on the moral side, better than the statesmen and philosophers of Rome and

Athens. The explanation is, perhaps, partly that Milton was an Arian, and therefore felt at liberty to emphasize the Jewish limitations of Christ : limitations the possibility of which, as recent controversies have shown, even Athanasian opinion has been forced to face. But, in any case, in the *Paradise Regained* stress is necessarily, for dramatic purposes, laid on the Hebrew and Messianic character of Christ, and from that point of view it is not unnatural to make Him the spokesman of Hebrew resistance to the intellectual encroachments of Greece and Rome. Another part of the explanation is that the strong Biblical and Hebraic element in Milton's character does seem to have increased in strength during his later years. It was far from getting exclusive possession even then, and all the evidence shows that he was always the very opposite of the narrow-minded Puritan fanatics of his day. But his tendencies in that direction would be exaggerated while he was occupied with a purely Biblical subject. And he may have thought, if he thought about the question at all, that the contemptuous tone adopted about classical culture in the speech of Christ was not only dramatically defensible, but balanced by the far finer passage, evidently written from his

heart, in which Satan exalts the glories of
Athens. It is, perhaps, the most famous
thing in the poem.

" Look once more, ere we leave this specular
      mount,
   Westward, much nearer by south-west;
      behold
   Where on the Ægean shore a city stands,
   Built nobly, pure the air and light the soil—
   Athens, the eye of Greece, mother of arts
   And eloquence, native to famous wits
   Or hospitable, in her sweet recess,
   City or suburban, studious walks and shades.
   See there the olive-grove of Academe,
   Plato's retirement, where the Attic bird
   Trills her thick-warbled notes the summer
      long;
   There flow'ry hill Hymettus, with the sound
   Of bees' industrious murmur, oft invites
   To studious musing; there Ilissus rolls
   His whispering stream. Within the walls
      then view
   The schools of ancient sages, his who bred
   Great Alexander to subdue the world,
   Lyceum there; and painted Stoa next.
   There thou shalt hear and learn the secret
      power
   Of harmony, in tones and numbers hit
   By voice or hand, and various-measured
      verse,
   Æolian charms and Dorian lyric odes,
   And his who gave them breath, but higher
      sung,

Blind Melesigenes, thence Homer called,
Whose poem Phœbus challenged for his own.
Thence what the lofty grave Tragedians
  taught
In chorus or iambic, teachers best
Of moral prudence, with delight received
In brief sententious precepts, while they
  treat
Of fate, and chance, and change in human
  life,
High actions and high passions best de-
  scribing."

It is plainly the very voice of the poet himself, and he may have felt certain that we
should so understand it. But it is difficult
not to regret that it is the Devil who is made
to pay Milton's great debt to Athens and
Christ who is made to repudiate it.

Yet, in spite of all this, in spite of its disdain
of the obvious attractions open to poetry, in
spite of much in it that alienates the sym-
pathies of many, the *Paradise Regained* has
received very high praise from the finest
judges of English poetry. Johnson and
Wordsworth have already been quoted, and
to them may be added Coleridge, who says
of it that " in its kind it is the most perfect
poem extant," and Mr. Mackail, who has
spoken of its " unique poetic qualities."
Why have the poets and critics been so much

more favourable to it than the public? Perhaps because artists are always inclined to value work in proportion to its difficulties. Indeed, this fallacy seems natural to all classes of men about their own work. Gardeners in England tend to admire a man who grows indifferent oranges more than a man who grows good strawberries. It is like what Johnson said of the preaching lady : " Sir, a woman's preaching is like a dog's walking on his hinder legs. It is not done well; but you are surprised to find it done at all." This tendency to let surprise sit in the seat which belongs to judgment is greatly intensified by professional knowledge. The architect is apt to exaggerate the merit of a building placed on a very awkward site, the artist to think a piece of very difficult foreshortening more beautiful than it really is. The public may not be so good a judge either of the building or of the drawing : but, knowing nothing of the technical difficulties, it at least forms its judgment on the true criterion which is, of course, the value of the product, not the surprisingness of its having been produced or the difficulties overcome in its production.

Something of this kind may account for the fact that *Paradise Regained* has been more appreciated by the poets than by the public.

The public finds it rather bare and dry and judges accordingly. The poets know how infinitely hard a task it was that Milton set himself, and find no praise too great for the man who did not fail in it. They see a poem of two thousand lines whose single subject is the attempt of a devil who knows himself doomed tr, defeat to persuade a divine Person who knows Himself assured of victory to be false to the law of His being. And into this barren theme they see art and nature, ethics and politics, luxury and splendour and empire, cunningly interwoven and

"Eden raised in the waste Wilderness."

They see a style stripped of almost all ornament especially in the speeches of our Lord : the poet deliberately walking always on the very edge of the gulf of prose and yet always as one perfectly assured that into that gulf his feet can never fall. Here and there, as when we come upon such lines as

"I never liked thy talk, thy offers less,"

we are nervous as we watch : but the poet passes on his way serenely unconscious of our fears, and in the very next speech is on the heights of poetry with the great description

of Athens. Once only, perhaps, in the reply
to Satan after the storm—

" Me worse than wet thou find'st not,"

we feel that the cunningly maintained balance
has failed and that the limit has been passed
which divides the severe from the grotesque.

The truth is that, if the narrowness of its
subject and the austerity of its style be
admitted, *Paradise Regained* is a poetic
achievement as great as it is surprising. It
cannot be *Paradise Lost*, of course, and that
is the fault for which it has not been forgiven.
And its fine things are even less evident, much
less evident, at a first reading than those of
Paradise Lost. But Milton has left nothing
more Miltonic. He did greater things but
nothing in which he stands so entirely alone.
There is no poem in English, perhaps none in
any language of the world, which exhibits to
the same degree the inherent power of style
itself, in its naked essence, unassisted by any
of its visible accessories. There are in it, of
course, some passages of characteristic splendour, the banquet in the wilderness, the vision
of Rome, and others ; but a large part of the
poem is as bare as the mountains and, to
the luxurious and conventional, as bleak and
forbidding. Its grave Dorian music, scarcely

heard by the sensual ear, is played by the mind to the spirit and by the spirit to the mind. Ever present as its art is, it is an art infinitely removed from that to which all the world at once responds and surrenders. It is not at first seen to be art at all. The verse which in truth dances so cunningly appears to the uninitiated to stumble and halt. The music, which the common ear is so slow to catch, makes us think of those Platonic mysteries of abstract number seen only in their perfection by some godlike mathematician who lives rapt above sense and matter in the contemplation of the Idea of Good.

But, if there is much in an art so consummate as Milton's which escapes analysis, there are also elements which can be measured and weighed. Here as in the *Paradise Lost* students of metre can count and compare his stresses and pauses, and set out some finite portion of the infinite variety of rhythms which, even more needed here than in *Paradise Lost*, sustains the poem in its difficult flight over so apparently barren a country. The art of the poet as distinct from the musician is less difficult to trace. An avowed sequel has to recall its predecessor and yet not to recall it too much. *Paradise Regained* recalls *Paradise Lost* by its central action, a tempta-

tion, by its council of devils, by its assembly
of the heavenly host, by a hundred echoes of
phrase and circumstance. But though the
heavenly host is itself unchanged, though it is
still the old " full frequence bright Of Angels "
yet there is now no real council. The Son,
the only spokesman who can address the
Father, is no longer present, and even the
hymn of the angels gets no more than a vague
description. A greater change has come over
the infernal council: scarcely any longer
infernal, for their leader can now open his
address to them with

"O ancient Powers of Air and this wide
World,"

and the meeting is held in mid air and no
longer in hell. Nor is any rivalry attempted
with the great debate of *Paradise Lost*: only
enough to awaken its memory in the reader
and to enable the poet to find a place in
the second meeting for the most obvious of
temptations which yet reverence forbade him
to introduce into the main action. And note
how this contains at least one of those small
dramatic touches for which, except from Mr.
Mackail, Milton has got too little credit.
Satan asks how he is to assail the new enemy :
and Belial, who stands for the sensualist man
of the world, at once offers his suggestion.

He is sure, as such men always are, that the lowest motive is invariably the true mainspring and explanation of all human actions : there is no beating about the bush with him : he is frank and cynical, and begins at once without shame, apology or preface—

" Set women in his eye and in his walk."

What could be more exactly in the downright manner affected by men of his type in the world of to-day and every day ? And there are other similar touches. Then again the sequel recalls its predecessor when we hear Satan strike the very note he struck so often in *Paradise Lost*—

" 'Tis true, I am that Spirit unfortunate,"

and when we see him fall in ruin at the awful end of the long debate—

" Now shew thy progeny; if not to stand
  Cast thyself down; safely, if Son of God;
  For it is written : ' He will give command
  Concerning thee to his Angels : in their
    hands
  They shall uplift thee, lest at any time
  Thou chance to dash thy foot against a
    stone.'
  To whom thus Jesus : Also it is written
  ' Tempt not the Lord thy God.' He said,
    and stood :
  But Satan, smitten with amazement, fell."

Nor must it be supposed by those who have not read the *Paradise Regained* that the bareness of its style is invariable. Most conspicuous, for reasons of reverence no doubt, in the speeches of Christ, it is far less marked in those of Satan and disappears altogether in some of the descriptive passages. Take, for instance, the famous temptation of the banquet—

" He spake no dream; for, as his words had end,
Our Saviour, lifting up his eyes, beheld
In ample space under the broadest shade,
A table richly spread in regal mode,
With dishes piled, and meats of noblest sort
And savour; beasts of chase, or fowl of game,
In pastry built, or from the spit, or boiled,
Grisamber-steamed; all fish from sea or
        shore
Freshet or purling brook, of shell or fin,
And exquisitest name, for which was drained
Pontus, and Lucrine bay, and Afric coast.
Alas, how simple, to these cates compared,
Was that crude apple that diverted Eve !
And at a stately sideboard, by the wine,
That fragrant smell diffused, in order stood
Tall stripling youths rich-clad, of fairer hue
Than Ganymed or Hylas; distant more,
Under the trees now tripped, now solemn
        stood,
Nymphs of Diana's train, and Naiades
With fruits and flowers from Amalthea's
        horn,

And ladies of the Hesperides, that seemed
Fairer than feigned of old, or fabled since
Of faery damsels met in forest wide
By knights of Logres, or of Lyones,
Lancelot, or Pelleas, or Pellenore."

Paradise Lost itself contains no more intricately beautiful passage than this. It is one of those things that have been the delight and despair of poets ever since. For all his disdain of the follies of the Middle Age Milton can never touch the old romances, as Joseph Warton well noted, without immediately rising into the most exquisite poetry: and this reluctant homage of classical genius is the greatest tribute ever paid to their undying fascination.

But of course such a passage as this is not typical of the poem: it is one of its far-shining heights which cannot be altogether missed even by eyes quite blind to the beauties of the lower country through which *Paradise Regained* takes the most part of its course. Ordinarily the poem is grave, plain and unadorned, engaged in the discussion of moral problems which give little opportunity for the more obvious graces of poetry. The interest of the speeches which constitute the bulk of it is threefold: technical, in the rhythmical or metrical skill by which Milton sustains an

abstract discourse expressed in unadorned
language and keeps it at the level of high
poetry; moral or intellectual, the interest
of the subjects discussed; and, the greatest
of all for many readers, autobiographical,
the interest of the evidence they afford of
the poet's own thoughts and character. All
may be seen, for instance, in such a confession
as that of Satan in the first book—

" Envy, they say, excites me, thus to gain
Companions of my misery and woe !
At first it may be; but, long since with woe
Nearer acquainted, now I feel by proof
That fellowship in pain divides not smart,
Nor lightens aught each man's peculiar load."

There is scarcely a word in it that prose cannot
use even to-day. The thought is one that
might come from any moralist; there is nothing
daring or imaginative about it. Yet out of
this what poetry Milton has made! The
personal emotion of it, the note of confession
and individual experience, has lifted it altogether above the level of the cold maxims
of the preacher who gives no sign of having
suffered, or sinned, or so much as lived, himself. Then the art of it : so entirely unperceived by the ordinary reader, so invincible
in its effect upon him. The whole secret of
it defies analysis : but a few ingredients can

be detected. There is comparatively little
of Milton's favourite alliteration : the tone
of the passage is too quiet for the free use of
an artistic device so instantly visible. But
note the beautiful line—

" Companions of my misery and woe "—

itself free flowing without a pause of any
kind, so as to prepare the better for the
full pause both of sense and of rhythm which
separates it from what follows. Then there
is the vivid conversational " At first it may
be," and its pause, contrasting so finely with
the next line where the pause is also after
the fifth syllable, but with a totally different
effect. Note again the variety of rhythm
which distinguishes the last two lines. Neither
has any strong pause in it : and they might
so easily have been a monotonous repetition.
Is it fanciful to think that, perhaps half unconsciously, Milton has suggested the quick
stab of pain or sorrow in the swift movement
of the first : and that the long-drawn rhythm
of the second is meant to convey something
of the dull years of misery which so often
follow?   Its first six syllables—

" Nor lightens aught each man's,"

if given their full effect of sound, take perhaps
half as long again to read as the first six of the

preceding line. In any case, whatever was
meant by it, the line is a most beautiful one in
itself, as well as full of one of the most moving
of human things, a strong man's confession
that his strength does not always suffice him.

These obviously autobiographical passages
are to be found all through the poem.   There
are the stately Roman embassies coming and
going in all their pomp : in which it is surely
Cromwell's Foreign Secretary who sees nothing
but

" tedious waste of time, to sit and hear
So many hollow compliments and lies,
Outlandish flatteries."

There is the old contempt of war and those
who in virtue of their victories

" swell with pride, and must be titled Gods,"

and of the mob who praise and admire

" they know not what,
And know not whom, but as one leads the
    other;
And what delight to be by such extolled,
To live upon their tongues and be their talk?
Of whom to be dispraised were no small praise,
His lot who dares be singularly good."

There is the contempt of wealth—

" Extol not riches then, the toil of fools,
The wise man's cumbrance, if not snare; "

a contempt which Milton shares with nearly all saints and heroes and most philosophers; a little ungratefully, perhaps, as if forgetting that, compared with the mass of men, he had himself always been rich, and that what he owed to the toil of his father had not proved in his case a snare or a cumbrance, but the necessary condition of the learning and the leisure he had used so nobly. Finally, to give no more instances, there is the confession at once so personal and so representative of the feeling of all men who have ever made the smallest effort to live well—

" Hard are the ways of truth, and rough to
        walk,
    Smooth on the tongue discoursed, pleasing
        to the ear,
    And tunable as sylvan pipe or song."

Who knows whether behind such words as these there lies the memory of some rapturous vision of the new world of love as St. Paul saw it, which had been cooled only too soon by humbling experience of the difficulty of " bearing all things " when all things included Salmasius, or an unthankful daughter?

This grave introspective note, present from the first in everything written by Milton and far more conspicuous in *Paradise Regained* than in *Paradise Lost*, is felt still more in the

last of his works, the drama *Samson Agonistes.*
It is in the Greek form with a Chorus : and
is as broodingly full as Æschylus or Sophocles
of the folly of man and the uncertainty and
sadness of human life; but Milton has added
an angry sternness of judgment on the one
hand, and on the other an assured faith in
divine deliverance, both of which are rather
Hebrew than Greek.   Into this strange drama,
so alien from all the literature of his day,
Milton has poured all the thoughts and
emotions with which the spectacle of his own
life filled him.   All through it we hear a faith
that was strong but never blind battling with
the spectacle of the wickedness of men and
the dark uncertainty of the ways of God.
The Philistines have triumphed, lords sit
" lordly in their wine " at Whitehall, the
Dagon of prelatism is once more enthroned
throughout the land, the saints are dispersed
and forsaken, and he himself, who had as he
thought so signally borne his witness for God,
sits blind and sad in his lonely house, " to
visitants a gaze Or pitied object," with no
hope left of high service to his country and
no prospect but that of a " contemptible old
age obscure."   No doubt he did not always
feel like that, for the evidence shows him
cheerful and friendly in company : and, of

course, the picture has undergone the imaginative heightening of art besides being coloured
by the story of Samson, so much sadder than
Milton's own. But the lonely hours of a
blind man of genius who has fought for a
great cause and been utterly defeated must
often be full of the hopeless half-resigned and
half-rebellious broodings in which throughout
Samson we hear so plainly the voice of Milton
himself.

" God of our fathers ! what is Man,
That thou towards him with hand so various—
Or might I say contrarious ?—
Temper'st thy providence through his short
        course ;
Not evenly, as thou rulest
The angelic orders and inferior creatures mute,
Irrational and brute ?
Nor do I name of men the common rout,
That wandering loose about
Grow up and perish as the summer fly,
Heads without name, no more remembered ;
But such as thou hast solemnly elected,
With gifts and graces eminently adorned,
To some great work, thy glory,
And people's safety, which in part they effect :
Yet toward these thus dignified thou oft,
Amidst their highth of noon,
Changest thy countenance and thy hand, with
        no regard
Of highest favours past
From thee on them, or them to thee of service."

This is Milton undisguised speaking of and for himself. And so is the still sadder outburst in the very first speech of Samson—

" O dark, dark, dark, amid the blaze of noon,
  Irrecoverably dark, total eclipse
  Without all hope of day !
  O first-created beam, and thou great Word,
  ' Let there be light, and light was over
    all ';
  Why am I thus bereaved thy prime decree ?
  The Sun to me is dark
  And silent as the Moon
  When she deserts the night,
  Hid in her vacant interlunar cave.
  Since light so necessary is to life,
  And almost life itself, if it be true
  That light is in the soul,
  She all in every part, why was the sight
  To such a tender ball as the eye confined,
  So obvious and so easy to be quenched,
  And not, as feeling, through all parts
    diffused,
  That she might look at will through every
    pore ?
  Then had I not been thus exiled from light,
  As in the land of darkness, yet in light,
  To live a life half dead, a living death,
  And buried; but, O yet more miserable !
  Myself my sepulchre, a moving grave;
  Buried, yet not exempt,
  By privilege of death and burial,
  From worst of other evils, pains, and wrongs,
  But made hereby obnoxious more

To all the miseries of life,
Life in captivity
Among inhuman foes."

This sublime music in which the soul's
emotion finds and obeys its own law was
scarcely audible to the age which followed
Milton's death, when poets had concentrated
all their art on the effort to make both
language and metre as instantaneously in-
telligible as possible. They succeeded much
better in the second task than in the first: for
the truth is that the exact meaning of a verse
is much more often difficult to ascertain in
the case of Pope than in the case of Milton.
But no one has ever doubted how to read
aloud a line of Pope or Dryden. And this
has obvious advantages and was, of course,
at first a great source of pleasure. It made
Pope's poetry the most immediately popular
we have ever had, as it still is the most effective for public quotation. Almost everybody,
as Mr. Bridges has said, " has a natural liking
for the common fundamental rhythms " and
" it is only after long familiarity with them
that the ear grows dissatisfied and wishes
them to be broken." But in poetry as in
music the more cultivated the ear the sooner
it gets tired of being given too little to do:
and as soon as every warbler had Pope's

tune by heart critical readers began to wish
for something less obvious. The ultimate
result of that dissatisfaction was the metrical
experiments of Coleridge and the rich harvest
of varied rhythms and melody with which
Shelley and Tennyson and Swinburne enriched
the nineteenth century. And all this movement had also, of course, a retrospective effect.
It may be true that, as Mr. Bridges says,
" there are very few persons indeed who take
such a natural delight in rhythm for its own
sake that they can follow with pleasure a
learned rhythm which is very rich in variety,
and the beauty of which is its perpetual freedom to obey the sense and diction;" but it
could not fail to be the case that their number
was increased by the comparative sensitive-
ness to the more intricate music of words
which was inevitably produced in those who
had learnt much Shelley or Tennyson by heart.
And such people at once heard things in
Milton which were absolutely inaudible to
the ears of Dr. Johnson's generation. The
comparative subtlety, both in imagination
and in form, of the poetry of the nineteenth
century made it impossible for poets to com-
pete with journalists for the attention of the
big public as Pope had done triumphantly;
but as a set off against that loss it gave a far

richer delight to those who were capable of
that interaction of the natural ear and the
spiritual to which all great poetry makes its
appeal. This led straight back to Milton who
made that double appeal as only a very few
poets in all the world have ever made it. And
the more poetry is studied and loved as the
greatest of the arts, as the medium through
which that combination of the vision of
genius with the slow trained cunning of the
craftsman, which is what great art is, finds
its most perfect expression, the more will men,
or at least Englishmen, return to Milton. And
especially, in some ways, to *Samson*, where
his art is at its boldest and freest, and where
it suffered longest from the indifference of
dull ears.

A little book of this kind is not the place
for a discussion of English metre, or even, in
any detail, of Milton's. Those who wish to
go into such studies will find much of what
they want in the Poet Laureate's book on
Milton's Prosody. It is possible to disagree
with some of his proposed scansions of doubtful
lines, but it is impossible not to learn a great
deal from suggestions as to the rhythmical
effects intended by Milton which come, as
these do, from one who is himself a master
of rhythm and has never concealed the fact

that Milton's was one of the schools in which
he passed his apprenticeship. So his analysis,
line by line, of the opening of the first chorus
of *Samson* will be a revelation to many of
what they have, perhaps, never felt at all, or
felt only unconsciously without understanding
anything of what it was which they felt or
why. But even without such help no one
whose ear has had the smallest training
can fail to notice some of the more daring
of Milton's metrical effects. In the lines
quoted above, for instance, who can miss the
triple stab of passionate agony in the thrice
repeated, strongly accented " dark, dark,
dark " ? The most careless reader cannot
fail to be arrested by the line, though he may
not realize the means employed by Milton
to enforce attention, the rare six stresses in
a ten-syllabled line, the still rarer effect of
three strongly stressed syllables following
immediately upon one another, the inversion
of three out of the five stresses of the next
line, "irrecoverably dark" suggesting the
spasmodic disorder of violent grief. These
are certainly devices deliberately chosen for
producing the required effects. And so,
probably, are the more regular rhythm of the
words which express the calming aspiration
up to the throne of God, and the quiet mono-

H

syllabic simplicity of the divine utterance,
" Let there be light," which continues its
softening influence over the return in the
following lines to his own sad conditions.
How smoothly the complaint now goes:
" The sun to me is dark And silent as the
moon." It is in comparison with the earlier
abruptness as if he had gone through something like the process of the psalmist, " until
I went into the sanctuary of God : then
understood I " what had before been " too
painful for me." Then there is the comparatively unmarked rhythm of the intellectual argumentative passage which follows :
till emotion begins again to overwhelm
reflection, and shows itself in the strong
alliteration of " light," " land," " light,"
" live," " life," " living," and in the strong
cæsura after " buried," the more marked for
coming so early in the verse.

Such poor noting of technicalities as this
gives, of course, no more of the secret of
Milton's wonderful poetry than anatomy gives
of the power and beauty of the human body.
But it has its interest and even its use : provided that too much importance is not attri-
buted to it and that no one makes the mistake
of the lady who, according to the story,
hopefully asked the painter what he mixed

his paints with, and received the crushing reply, " With my brains, Madam."

Samson Agonistes stands in marked contrast to its predecessor, *Paradise Regained*. And not only in being a drama. Its intense omnipresent emotion makes a still more important difference. In passing from one to the other we pass from the least to the most emotional of Milton's works. This would in any case have been a gain for most readers : but the gain is made more important by the extreme severity of Milton's final poetic manner. A style which excludes almost all ornament stands in especial need of the support of a visibly felt emotion. It has been said by a living writer that " when reason is subsidiary to emotion verse is the right means of expression, and, when emotion to reason, prose." This is roughly true, though the poetry of mere emotion is poor stuff. The special faculty of the poet, as Johnson well said, is that of joining music with reason. That is to say that the poet unites thought and feeling and gives them perfect expression. They are not distinct : they become in his hands a new single life, a unity. You cannot separate the emotion from the thought in any great line of poetry. When Wordsworth talks of the " unimaginable touch of time," there is

plainly emotion as well as thought and
memory in his words : when Shelley cries in
his despair—

" Fresh spring, and summer, and winter hoar,
  Move my faint heart with grief, but with
      delight
    No more—O never more ! "

it is no mere cry of the heart : the mind is in
it too : and neither in him nor in Wordsworth
can you get the two apart again after the
poet has joined them together.

Now, though in *Paradise Regained* the
intellect is not allowed, as in much eighteenth-
century poetry, to become so dominant as
to make us feel that prose and not verse was
the proper medium for what the poet had to
say, yet it does play a greater part than it
can commonly play with safety, perhaps a
greater part than it plays in any other English
poem of the first rank. It is only Milton's
unfailing gift of poetic style which saves the
situation. He could do what Wordsworth
could not : conduct long discussions on
abstract questions without descending from
the note of poetry to that of the lecture-room.
The gallant explorer who fights his way
through the *Prelude* and the *Excursion* wins,
as he deserves, a great reward, and a greater
still if he does it a second time and a third,

when he has learnt that they both have
marshy valleys into which he need not twice
descend.   But he has paid a price for the
lesson, paid it in the endurance of a great
deal of solid and heavy prose.   That is partly
because Wordsworth often thinks without
feeling or imagining : he gives us his thought
as it is in itself, as a professor of moral philosophy gives it, without passing it through the
transforming processes of the emotions and
the imagination.   These hardly fail Milton half
a dozen times in all his poetry : and the result
is the difference between such lines as—

" This is the genuine course, the aim, and end
 Of prescient reason; all conclusions else
 Are abject, vain, presumptuous, and per-
   verse : "

and such as Milton writes when he is nearest
to bare thinking—

      " Who therefore seeks in these
True wisdom, finds her not, or by delusion
Far worse, her false resemblance only meets,
An empty cloud."

The difference is also partly due to what,
indeed, is another side of the same distinction :
the fact that Wordsworth has not and Milton
has a constant possession of the great or
grand style.   This is plain in such passages
as those just quoted : it is plainer still where
the poets come close to each other in

descriptive passages : as, for instance, in
Wordsworth's—

"Negro ladies in white muslin gowns,"

and Milton's—

"Dusk faces with white silken turbans
    wreathed; "

between which yawns an obviously impassable
gulf.

Milton is sometimes harsh, crabbed, grim in
expression as in thought : but these things
are not at all necessarily fatal to poetry as is
the cool and contented obviousness of Wordsworth's weak moments. Milton is occasionally contented in his own lofty fashion, but
he is never cool, and never less so than in
Samson. All through it he is face to face
with a tremendous issue in which he himself is
supremely interested : he is " enacting hell,"
to use Goethe's curious phrase, which fits
Milton so much better than it fits the serenity
of Homer. Twenty years before he had
written, in quite another connection, " No
man knows hell like him who converses most
in heaven " : and now in his old age he
embodies that tremendous truth in his last
poem. All his poems are intensely emotional
and personal : but none so much so as *Samson
Agonistes,* where he is fixing all eyes on the

tragedy of his own life. The parallel between Samson and Milton does not extend, of course, to all the details. But even of them many correspond, such as the blindness, the disastrous marriage with " the daughter of an infidel," the old age of a broken and defeated champion of God become a gazing-stock to triumphant profanity. But more than any special circumstance it is the whole general position of Samson as a man dedicated from his birth to the service of God, and gladly accepting the dedication, yet failing in his task and apparently deserted by his God, which makes of him a type in which Milton can see himself and the Cromwellian saints who lie ground under the heels of the victorious Philistines of the Restoration. To him as to Samson the situation is one that makes questionings on the dark and doubtful ways of God unavoidable : darker to him even than to Samson : for he has no guilty memory of a supreme act of folly to explain the divine desertion.

The action of the drama is extremely simple. Samson is found enjoying a brief respite from his punishment. The day is a feast of Dagon, and the Philistine " superstition " allows no work to be done on it. Accordingly an attendant who is a mute person is leading

him to a bank where he is accustomed to take
what rest he is allowed and enjoy

" The breath of heaven fresh blowing, pure
        and sweet
  With day-spring born; "

that sensation of delicate scents and cool
breezes which, as Milton knew only too well,
mean so much more to the blind than to those
who can see. Then his restless thoughts
begin to crowd upon him—

" Why was my breeding ordered and pre-
        scribed
  As of a person separate to God,
  Designed for great exploits ? "

The whole passage belongs naturally enough
to Samson : but obviously here, as well as in
the blindness, the poet is already thinking of
himself. So again, when Samson proceeds to
speak of being

                              " exposed
To daily fraud, contempt, abuse, and wrong,"

one can scarcely miss a reference to the
daughters who purloined and sold the blind
father's books. When the soliloquy draws
to an end the Chorus, men of his tribe, come
to visit Samson. Not even Milton ever made
the arrangement and sound of words do more
to enforce their meaning than he does in this
wonderful opening chorus—

" This, this is he; softly a while;
Let us not break in upon him.
O change beyond report, thought, or belief!"

They chant their inevitable wonder at the
contrast between what Samson was and what
he is.

" O mirror of our fickle state,
Since man on earth, unparalleled!
The rarer thy example stands,
By how much from the top of wondrous
glory,
Strongest of mortal men,
To lowest pitch of abject fortune thou art
fallen."

No reader of Greek can fail to be reminded
of more than one chorus in the *Œdipus* of
Sophocles—

ἰὼ γενεαὶ βροτῶν
ὡς ὑμᾶς ἴσα καὶ τὸ μηδὲν ζώσας ἐναριθμῶ—

" Alas, ye generations of men, how utterly
a thing of nought I count the life ye have
to live! For what man is there who wins
more of happiness than just the seeming and
after the semblance a falling away. With
thy fate before mine eyes, unhappy Œdipus, I
can call no earthly creature blest." Here and
there, as in this passage, the parallel is very
close. But Milton's genius is too great and
self-reliant for mere imitation. He sometimes
recalls the very words of Greek poets as he

H 2

does those of the Bible : but that is not
because he is artificially imitating either, but
because he has assimilated the spirit of both
and made them a part of himself.

The Chorus express their sympathy with
Samson and he replies, bitterly reproaching
his own folly and that of the rulers of Judah
who gave him up to their enemies. But
human blindness will not ultimately defeat
the ways of God : and the Chorus sing their
song of faith, in which rhyme is called in to
give its touch of impatient contempt at the
folly of the atheist.

" Just are the ways of God,
     And justifiable to men;
     Unless there be who think not God at all.
     If any be, they walk obscure;
     For of such doctrine never was there school,
     But the heart of the fool,
     And no man therein doctor but himself."

So ends the first act or episode of the
drama.   The second is the visit of Samson's
father Manoah, whose cry is—

" Who would be now a father in my stead ? "

He is trying to negotiate for his son's ransom :
but Samson refuses, not desiring life, desiring
rather to pay the full penalty of his sin.   He
cannot share his father's hopes that God will
give him back the sight he so misused—

" All otherwise to me my thoughts portend,
  That these dark orbs no more shall treat
    with light,
  Nor the other light of life continue long,
  But yield to double darkness nigh at hand :
  So much I feel my genial spirits droop,
  My hopes all flat; Nature within me seems
  In all her functions weary of herself;
  My race of glory run, and race of shame,
  And I shall shortly be with them that rest."

So Manoah leaves him, and in a noble lyric
he laments over his greatest sufferings, which
are not those of the body but those of the
mind—
              " which no cooling herb
  Or med'cinal liquor can assuage,
  Nor breath of vernal air from snowy Alp."

A choral song on the mysterious dealings
of God closes this episode which is followed
by the most dramatically effective in the
poem, that of the visit of Dalila.   The moment
the blind man is told that it is " Dalila, thy
wife," he cries—

" My wife ! my traitress ! let her not come
    near me : "

and his reply to her offer of penitence, affection and help, begins with the daringly
expressive line—

" Out, out, hyæna ! these are thy wonted arts."

A long and telling debate follows, in which

Dalila makes very good points, one of them recalling the scene in which Eve reproaches Adam for indulging her instead of exercising his right to command and control the weakness of her sex. To this argument Dalila receives the stern, characteristically Miltonic reply—

"All wickedness is weakness: that plea, therefore
With God or man will gain thee no remission,"

He refuses her intercession with the Philistine lords, forbids her even to touch his hand;

"Not for thy life, lest fierce remembrance wake
My sudden rage to tear thee joint by joint,"

and drives her to remind him defiantly that, whatever he and his Hebrews may say of her, she appeals to another tribunal of fame—

"In Ecron, Gaza, Asdod, and in Gath,
I shall be named among the famousest
Of women, sung at solemn festivals,
Living and dead recorded."

So she goes out, and the Chorus make Miltonic meditations on the unhappiness of marriage and the divinely appointed subjection of women.

The next visitor is Harapha, the Philistine giant, who comes to taunt Samson, and is defied by him to mortal combat. This episode is perhaps the least interesting, but it advances the action by exhibiting Samson's returning sense that God is still with him and will yet do some great work through him. It fitly leads to the chorus—

> " O, how comely it is, and how reviving
> To the spirits of just men long oppressed,
> When God into the hands of their deliverer
> Puts invincible might,
> To quell the mighty of the earth, the
> oppressor,
> The brute and boisterous force of violent
> men,
> Hardy and industrious to support
> Tyrannic power, but raging to pursue
> The righteous and all such as honour truth!"

In the next scene an officer comes to demand Samson's presence at the feast of Dagon that he may entertain the Philistine lords with feats of strength. He at first dismisses the messenger with a contemptuous refusal : but, with a premonition of the end which recalls Œdipus at Colonus, he suddenly changes his mind—

> " I begin to feel
> Some rousing motions in me, which dispose
> To something extraordinary my thoughts.
>   .   .   .   .
> If there be aught of presage in the mind,
> This day will be remarkable in my life
> By some great act, or of my days the last."

" Go, and the Holy One
Of Israel be thy guide,"

sing the Chorus : and he leaves the scene, like
Œdipus, to return no more, but to be more
felt in his absence than in his presence.
Manoah re-enters to utter his further hopes
of ransom, in which there is a note of Sopho-
clean irony recalling the ignorant optimism
of Œdipus in the *Tyrannus*; and as he and
the Chorus talk they hear at first a loud
shouting, apparently of triumph, and then
another louder and more terrible—

Manoah.
                              " O what noise !
Mercy of Heaven ! what hideous noise was
          that ?
Horribly loud, unlike the former shout."

Chorus.
" Noise call you it, or universal groan,
    As if the whole inhabitation perished ? "

They dare not enter the city : and, as they
speculate on what this great event can be,
a Hebrew spectator of the catastrophe comes
up and, after some brief exchange of question
and answer exactly in the manner of the Greek
tragedians, tells the whole story at length.
The end has come. Samson is dead, but
death is swallowed up in victory : what has
happened is the last and most tremendous

triumph of the divinely chosen hero whose
death is more fatal to his country's enemies
than even his life had been. There is nothing
left to do but to close the drama, as most
Greek tragedies close, with a brief choral song
of submission to the divine governance of the
world:

" All is best, though we oft doubt
What the unsearchable dispose
Of Highest Wisdom brings about,
And ever best found in the close.
Oft He seems to hide his face,
But unexpectedly returns,
And to his faithful champion hath in place
Bore witness gloriously; whence Gaza
    mourns,
And all that band them to resist
His uncontrollable intent.
His servants He, with new acquist
Of true experience from this great event,
With peace and consolation hath dismissed,
And calm of mind, all passion spent."

Such is Milton's drama: a thing worth
dwelling on as entirely unique in any modern
language. Some good judges have thought
it the finest of his works. That will not be
admitted if poetry is to be judged either by
universality of appeal or by extent and
variety of range. *L'Allegro* and *Il Penseroso*
will always have far more readers: and
Paradise Lost embraces an immeasurably

greater span of human life. But, if not the greatest, *Samson* is probably for its own audience the most moving of Milton's works. It is not everybody who has in him the grave emotions to which it appeals : but whoever has will find them stirred by *Samson* as few other books in all the literature of the world can stir them.

It is curious to think of Milton composing such a drama in the midst of the theatrical revival of the Restoration. Did ever poet set himself in such opposition to the literary current of his day? Dryden's unbounded admiration for him is well known : but he understood the genius of *Paradise Lost* so little as to make an opera out of it, and he must have understood even less of *Samson*. The drama was then so much the most fashionable form of literature that he may have felt that in writing *The State of Innocence* and its preface he was taking the best means of directing public attention to *Paradise Lost*. But he would scarcely have tried to do the same for *Samson*. He had wished, perhaps, as Mr. Verrall has suggested, to write an epic and had failed to do so : hence his profound reverence for the man who had not failed. But he had written many dramas and here he had succeeded : he had pleased both his

contemporaries and himself. He would feel
no need there to take lessons from Milton.
Nor is he to be blamed. He and his fellow
dramatists are justly criticized for many
things, but there is nothing to complain of
in their unlikeness to Milton. They wrote
for the stage. He avowedly did not. They
wrote in the spirit of the theatre of their day,
with the object of providing themselves with
a little money and " the town " with a few
hours of more or less intellectual amusement.
He wrote out of his own mind and soul, not
for the entertainment of the idle folk of his
own or any other day, but for men who in
all times and countries should prove capable
of knowing a great work when they saw it.
Besides, his contemporary dramatists followed,
quite legitimately, the theatrical traditions
of England or France : he the very different
dramatic system of the Greeks. His drama
is what Greek tragedies were, an act of
religion. It could take its place quite naturally, as they did, as part of a great national
religious festival performed on a holy day.
It is like them in the solemn music of its
utterance : in its deep sense of the gravity
of the issues on which human life hangs. It
is like them also in technical points such as
the use of a Chorus to give expression to the

spectator's emotions, the paucity of actors present on the stage at any moment, the curious
imitation, to be seen also in *Comus*, of the
Greek *stichomuthia*, in which a verbal passage
of arms is conducted on the principle of giving
each speaker one line for his attack or retort.

There are, indeed, some fundamental differences. They are important enough to have
led so great a critic as Professor Jebb to
argue that Milton's drama is too Hebrew to
be Hellenic at all. His point is that Greek
tragedy aims at producing an imaginative
pleasure by arousing a " sense, on the one
hand, of the heroic in man; on the other
hand, of a superhuman controlling power ";
and he asserts that this is not the method
adopted by Milton in *Samson*. Samson is
throughout a free man; his misfortunes are
the fruit of his own folly. God is still on his
side and his death is a patriotic triumph, not,
like the death of Heracles, who resembles him
in so many ways, merely the final proof of
the all-powerful malignity of fate.

No one will venture to differ from Jebb
on such a question without a sense of great
temerity. But perhaps the truth is that
one who had lived all his life, as Jebb had,
in the closest intimacy with the Greek drama,
would be apt to feel small differences from

it too much and broad resemblances too little. To the shepherd all his sheep differ from each other : the danger for him is to forget, what the ignorant stranger sees, that they are also all very much alike. So Jebb is no doubt perfectly right in the distinction he makes : but he is surely blinded by his own knowledge when he argues from it that *Samson Agonistes* " is a great poem and a noble drama; but neither as poem nor as drama is it Hellenic." Of that question comparative ignorance is perhaps a better judge. For it can still see that the broad division which separates the world's drama into two kinds is a real thing, and that Milton's drama belongs in spite of differences unquestionably to the Greek kind and not to the other, both by its method and by its spirit. There can be no real doubt that it is far more like the *Prometheus* or the *Œdipus* than it is like *Hamlet* or *All for Love*. Probably no great tragedy of any sort can be made without that sense of the contrast between man's will and the " superhuman controlling power " of which Jebb speaks as peculiarly Greek. Certainly it is present in the greatest of Shakspeare's tragedies, and not seldom finds open expression. " There's a divinity that shapes our ends."

But the point is that in *Samson*, the note of which is always the classical, never the mystical or romantic, this sense is present, not in Shakspeare's way, but substantially in the Greek way. The fact that Samson is free and that his God is his friend does not prevent his feeling just in the Greek way that God's ways are dark and inscrutable, past man's finding out, and far above out of the reach of his control. It does not prevent his being helpless as well as heroic, fully conscious that all his strength leaves him still a weak child at the absolute disposal of incomprehensible Omnipotence. So the whole atmosphere of the play, as well as its formal mould, will always recall the Greek tragedies. And rightly : the likenesses of every kind are far greater than the differences. The distinctions which led Jebb to declare it was not Hellenic at all are far less important than the kinship which made a still greater critic, the poet Goethe, declare that it had " more of the antique spirit than any production of any other modern poet."

A more obvious and perhaps more important difference than that on which Jebb lays such stress is, of course, the fundamental one that the Greek plays were written for performance and that many of them have

elaborately contrived " plots." No one supposes that *Samson* would be effective on the
stage; but the modern dramatist who could
make his play as exciting to the spectator as
the *Œdipus Tyrannus* or *Electra* of Sophocles,
or the *Hippolytus* or *Medea* of Euripides,
would assuredly be no ordinary playwright.
This Milton did not attempt. His drama
resembles rather the earlier Greek tragedies
where the lyrical element is still the principal
thing while the " plot " and the persons who
act its story play a comparatively subordinate
part. It is, at any rate in form, more like
Æschylus than Sophocles, and more like the
Persæ and the *Prometheus* than the Oresteian
Trilogy. To the *Prometheus*, indeed, it bears
particularly close and obvious resemblances;
for instance, both have a heroic and defiant
prisoner as their principal figure, and as their
minor figures a succession of friends and
enemies who visit him.

However, literary parallels and precedents
of this kind are perhaps rather interesting
than important. Milton's greatness is his
own. Only the fact remains that, as it was
of an order that need not fear to measure
itself with the Greeks and as he happened to
put its dramatic expression into a Greek form,
he has given us something which comes far

nearer to producing on us the particular
impression of sublimity made by the greatest
Greek dramas than anything else in English or
perhaps in any modern language. In English
nothing worth mentioning of the kind has
been attempted, till in our own day Mr.
Bridges wrote his beautiful *Prometheus the
Fire-Giver* and *Achilles in Scyros*. But, characteristic and therefore partly Miltonic as
these are, they make no pretence to rival
Samson Agonistes. They are altogether on a
smaller scale of art, of thought, of emotion.

Samson Agonistes is Milton's last word and
on the whole his saddest. Yet the final effect
of great art is never sad. The sense of greatness transcends all pain. In the preface of
Samson Milton alludes to Aristotle's remark
that it is the function of tragedy to effect
through pity and fear a proper purgation of
these emotions. Whatever be the precise
meaning of that famous and disputed sentence,
there is no doubt that Milton gives part of its
general import truly enough when he paraphrases it " to temper and reduce them to just
measure with a kind of delight stirred up by
reading or seeing those passions well imitated."
And its application extends far beyond the
mere field of tragedy. So far as other kinds
of poetry, or indeed any of the arts, deal with

subjects that arouse any of the deeper human
emotions, the law of purification by a kind
of delight is one by which they stand or fall.
A crucifixion which is merely painful, as
many primitive crucifixions are, or merely
disgusting, as many later ones are, is so far
a failure. It has not done the work art has
to do. Shakspeare knew this well enough,
though he very likely never thought about it.
The final word of his great tragedies is one of
sorrow overpassed and transformed. "The
rest is silence;" "Dost thou not see my
baby at my breast That sucks the nurse
asleep?" "I have almost forgot the taste
of fears;" "My heart doth joy that yet in
all my life I found no man but he was true to
me!" This is the note always struck before
the very end comes. And Milton, so unlike
Shakspeare both as man and as artist, is no
less conspicuous than he in the strict observ-
ance of this practice. All his poems, without
exception, end in quietness and confidence.
The beauty of the last lines of *Paradise Lost*,
to which early critics were so strangely blind,
is now universally celebrated—

"Some natural tears they dropped, but wiped
    them soon;
The world was all before them, where to
    choose

> Their place of rest, and Providence their
>   guide.
> They, hand in hand, with wandering steps
>   and slow,
> Through Eden took their solitary way."

The storm and stress of day are over and are
followed by the passionless quiet of evening.
So in *Paradise Regained*. A modern poet
would have been tempted to end at line 635,
with a kind of dramatic fall of the curtain—

>   " on thy glorious work
> Now enter, and begin to save Mankind."

Not so Milton. As after the most awe-
inspiring death known to literature the
Œdipus Coloneus closes on the note of
acquiescent peace—

> " Come, cease lamentation, lift it up no more;
>   for verily these things stand fast; "

so Milton ends the long debate of his poem, not
with victory, but with silence—

>   " He, unobserved,
> Home to his mother's house private re-
>   turned."

It is indeed just the opposite in one way
of the conclusion of *Paradise Lost*. The man
and woman who had fallen before the Tempter
had no home to return to : they must seek a
new " place of rest " elsewhere in the new
world that was before them. The Man who

had vanquished him could go back quietly
to the home of his childhood. But the contrast is external, the likeness essential. For
the first man as well as the second there is
an appointed place of rest and a Providence
to guide : the two poems can both end on
the same note of that peace which follows
upon the right understanding of all great
experiences.

This, which is only implied in his earlier
poems, is almost expressly set forth in the
last of all Milton's words, the already quoted
conclusion of Samson—

> " His servants He, with new acquist
> Of true experience from this great event,
> With peace and consolation hath dismissed,
> And calm of mind, all passion spent."

Milton was a passionate man who lived in
passionate times. Neither his passions nor
those of the men of his day are of very much
matter to us now. But the art in which he
" spent " them, in which, that is to say, he
embodied, transcended and glorified them,
till through it he and we alike attain to consolation and calm, is an eternal possession
not only of the English race but of the whole
world.

BIBLIOGRAPHY

THE literature that in one way or another deals with Milton is, of course, immense. His name fills more than half of one of the volumes of the great British Museum Catalogue, more than sixteen pages being devoted to the single item of *Paradise Lost*. They afford perhaps the most striking of all proofs of the universality of his genius; for they include translations into no fewer than eighteen languages, many of which possess a large choice of versions. Into more than a very small fraction of such a vast field it is obviously impossible to enter here. Only a few notes can be given, under the four headings of Poetry, Prose, Biography and Criticism.

POETRY

Of the poetry, it may be worth saying, though MSS. hardly come within the scope of a brief bibliography of this sort, that a manuscript, mainly in the handwriting of Milton himself and containing many of his early poems, is preserved in the Library of Trinity College, Cambridge. The printed copies, of course, begin with those published in his own lifetime. They contain practically the whole of his poetry. The most important are the volume containing his early poems issued in 1645, *Paradise Lost* which first appeared in 1667, *Paradise Regained* and *Samson Agonistes* which followed in 1671, and a re-issue in 1673, with additions, of the volume of his minor poems already printed in 1645. The first complete edition was *The Poetical Works of Mr. John Milton,* issued by Jacob Tonson in 1695.

So much for the bare text. Annotation naturally soon followed. The earliest commentator was Patrick Hume who published an edition of the poems with notes on *Paradise Lost* in 1695. But the most famous, though also least important, of Milton's early critics was the greatest of English scholars, Richard Bentley, who in 1732 issued an edition of *Paradise Lost* in which whole passages were relegated to the margin as the spurious interpolations of an imaginary editor. Such a book is, of course, merely a curiosity connecting two

250

great names. The real beginning in the work of editing Milton as a classic should be edited was made by Thomas Newton, afterwards Bishop of Bristol, who in 1749 brought out an edition of *Paradise Lost*, "with Notes of Various Authors," and followed it in 1752 with a similar volume including *Paradise Regained* and the minor poems. Newton's work was often reprinted, and remained the standard edition till it was superseded by that of the Rev. H. J. Todd which first appeared in 1801. The final issue of Todd is that of 1826 in six volumes which, in spite of many notes which are defective, many which are antiquated and some which are superfluous, may still claim to be the best library edition of Milton. Among the best of those which have appeared since are Thomas Keightley's, published in 1859, which contains excellent notes, and Prof. David Masson's, which is the work of the most learned and devoted of all Milton's editors. Both of these have the advantage of Todd in some respects; Keightley in acuteness and penetration, Masson in completeness of knowledge. But no single editor's work can be a perfect substitute for a *variorum* edition like that of Todd, giving the comments and suggestions of many different minds. The most complete edition of Masson's work is the final library one in three volumes, 1890; there is also a convenient smaller issue, based on this, but omitting some of its editorial matter. It was last printed in three volumes 1893. It contains a Memoir, rather elaborate Introductions to all the poems, an Essay on Milton's English and Versification, and reduced Notes.

A text with Critical Notes by W. Aldis Wright was issued by the Cambridge University Press in one volume, 1903. The text of the earliest printed editions of the several poems was reprinted in 1900 in an edition prepared for the Clarendon Press by the Rev. H. C. Beeching.

It may be worth while adding that Milton's Latin and Italian poems were translated by the poet Cowper and printed in 1808 by his biographer, Hayley, in a beautiful quarto volume with designs by Flaxman. These translations are reprinted in the "Aldine" edition of Milton, 1826. Masson has also given translations of most of them in his *Life of Milton* and in his 1890 library edition of the Poems.

PROSE

The Prose works were, of course, mostly issued as books or pamphlets in Milton's lifetime. They were collected by Toland in three volumes *folio*, 1698. There are several more modern editions; as that published in 1806 in seven volumes with a *Life* by Charles Symmons; that of Pickering, who included them in his fine eight-volume edition, *The Works of John Milton in Verse and Prose, Edited by John Mitford, 1851;* and that in Bohn's Standard Library, in six volumes, edited, with some notes of a somewhat controversial character, by J. A. St. John, 1848. The first volume of a new edition edited by Sir Sidney Lee appeared in 1905. One of the most curious of the prose works, the *De Doctrina Christiana* or *Treatise of Christian Doctrine,* was not known till 1823, when it was discovered in the State Paper Office. It was edited, with an English translation, by the Rev. C. R. Sumner in 1825 and is included in Bohn's edition.

BIOGRAPHY

The earliest sources for the biography of Milton, outside his own works, are the account given in the *Fasti Oxonienses* of Anthony à Wood, 1691, the *Brief Lives* of John Aubrey, and the Life prefixed by the poet's nephew, Edward Phillips, to an edition of the *Letters of State,* printed in 1694. A very large number of Lives of Milton have been written since, based on these materials and those collected from a few other sources. The most famous and in some ways the best, in spite of its unfairness, is that of Johnson, to be found in his *Lives of the Poets.* The best short modern Life is Mark Pattison's masterly, though occasionally wilful, little book in the English Men of Letters Series. For the library and for students all other biographies have been superseded by the great work of David Masson, who spared no labours to investigate every smallest detail of the life of Milton and to place the whole in the setting of an elaborate history of England in Milton's day. The value of the book is somewhat impaired by the very strong Puritan and anti-Cavalier partisanship of the writer; and its style suffers from an imitation of Carlyle. But nothing can seriously detract from the immense debt every student of Milton owes to the author of this monumental biography which appeared in seven volumes, 1859–1894.

An interesting critical discussion of the various portraits representing or alleged to represent Milton is prefixed to the Catalogue of the Exhibition held at Christ's College Cambridge during the Milton Tercentenary in 1908. It is by Dr. G. C. Williamson.

CRITICISM

A poet at once so learned and so great as Milton inevitably invited criticism. The first and most generous of his critics was his great rival Dryden, who, in a few words of the preface to *The State of Innocence*, published the year after Milton's death, led the note of praise, which has been echoed ever since by speaking of *Paradise Lost* as " one of the greatest, most noble and most sublime poems which either this age or nation has produced." The next great name in the list is that of Addison, who contributed a series of papers on Milton to the *Spectator* in 1712. Like all criticism except the work of the supreme masters, they are written too exclusively from the point of view of their own day to retain more than a small fraction of their value after two hundred years have passed. But they are of considerable historical interest and may still be read with pleasure, like everything written by Addison. A less sympathetic but finer piece of work is the critical part of Johnson's famous *Life*. It is full of crudities of every sort, such as the notorious remark that " no man could have fancied that he read *Lycidas* with pleasure had he not known the author"; and perhaps nothing Johnson ever wrote displayed more nakedly the narrow limits of his appreciation of poetry. But, in spite of all its defects, it exhibits its writer's great gifts; and its absolute and unshrinking sincerity, its half-reluctant utterance of some of the truest praise ever spoken of Milton, its profound knowledge of the way in which the human mind approaches both literature and life, will always preserve it as one of the most interesting criticisms which Milton has provoked. Johnson's friend, Thomas Warton, in his edition of the minor poems issued in 1785, led the way to an understanding of much in Milton to which Johnson and his school were entirely blind. This movement has continued ever since, and is seen in the immense influence Milton had upon the poets of the nineteenth century, especially upon Wordsworth and Keats; an influence of exactly the opposite sort to that which he exercised with such disastrous effect upon many poets of the century immediately succeeding his own. It is also seen in the finer intelligence of the critical studies of his work. These are far too many to mention here. Among the best are Hazlitt's Lecture on Shakspeare and Milton in his *Lectures on the English Poets ;* Matthew Arnold's speech at the unveiling of a Milton memorial, printed in the second series of his *Essays in Criticism;* Sir Walter Raleigh's volume, *Milton,* published in 1900, and *The Epic,* by Lascelles Abercrombie, 1914, which is full of fine and suggestive criticism of Milton. *Milton's Prosody by Robert Bridges, 1901,* is the best study of the metre and scansion of Milton's later poems, especially of *Paradise Lost.*

INDEX TO PRINCIPAL PERSONS, PLACES, AND WORKS MENTIONED

ABERCROMBIE, L., 136–7, 253
Absalom and Achitophel, 105
Achilles in Scyros, 246
Addison, Joseph, 77, 253
Adonais, 125
Ad Patrem, 39–40.
Æneid, The, 150, 175, 196
Æschylus, 245
À Kempis, Thomas, 147
Aldersgate Street, 46
All for Love, 243
Allegro, L', 41, 70, 93, 99, 106 et sqq., 123, 239
Anglesey, Earl of, 72, 82
Annesley, Arthur, 72
Aquinas, Thomas, 157
Arbuthnot, Epistle to, 105
Arcades, 41, 42
Arcadia, 58
Areopagitica, 44, 49, 64
Arianism, 204
Ariosto, 153
Aristotle, 86, 200
Arnold, Matthew, 164, 253
Arthurian Epic (planned), 45, 148–9
At a Solemn Music, 13, 42, 97, 100, 103, 147
Athens, 205–6, 209
Aubrey, John, 29, 252

Barbican, the, 54
Baroni, Leonora, 44–5
Barrow, Samuel, 82
Beeching, Rev. H. C., 251
Bentley, Richard, 250
Bibliography, 250–3
Blake, Admiral, 57
Bohn's Standard Library, 252
Bow Church, 25
Bread Street, 24, 75
Bridges, Robert, 26, 108, 222, 223, 246, 253
Brief Lives, 252
Buckingham, Duke of, 58
Byron, Lord, 90

Cambridge, 28, 29, 30, 31–7, 39, 42, 85, 120, 121, 124, 250, 252
Carlyle, Thomas, 252

Caroline, Queen, 77
Charles I, 11, 28, 58, 59, 60, 63, 64, 67, 71, 86
Charles II, 47, 60, 65, 71, 72, 73, 82, 86
Chaucer, Geoffrey, 90, 111
Christina, Queen of Sweden, 60
Christ's College, Cambridge, 28, 29, 120, 121, 124, 252
Clarendon, Earl of, 73
Clarges, Sir Thomas, 72
Coleridge, S. T., 206
Comus, 13, 41, 42, 95, 100, 110, 112–13 et sqq., 128, 242
Constable, 135
Coriolanus, 85
Cowper, William, 69, 251
Criticisms, 252–3
Cromwell, Oliver, 55, 57, 63, 64, 67, 68, 69, 71, 133, 139, 176

Dante, 10, 11–12, 33, 120, 153–7
Daphnaïda, 125
Davenant, William, 72
Defensio Regia, 60, 61
Defensio Secunda, 61
De Quincey, Thomas, 96
Diodati, Charles, 42, 124, 125
Divina Commedia, La, 120, 157
Divorce pamphlets, 50 et sqq.
Doctrina Christiana, De, 252
Dorset, Earl of, 81
Dowland, Robert, 28
Drayton, Michael, 124
Drummond, William, 124, 135
Dryden, John, 80–2, 90, 103, 104–5, 117, 240, 253

Eikon Basilike, the, 57–8
Eikonoklastes, 58, 61
Electra, The, 245
Elizabeth, Queen, 85
English Men of Letters Series, 252
Epic, The, 253
Epigrams, Latin, on La Baroni, 45
Epitaph on the Marchioness of Winchester, 36, 37, 97, 103
Epitaphium Damonis, 124
Essays in Criticism, 253
Euripides, 77, 82, 245
Excursion, The, 136, 228–9

254

Faerie Queen, The, 115
Fairfax, General, 139, 171
Faithful Shepherdess, The, 115
Fasti Oxonienses, 252
Faust, 196
Fire of London, 75
Flaxman, John, 251
Fletcher, John, 107, 115
Florence, 43, 44, 46
France, 43, 46, 59

Galileo, 44, 45
Gerusalemme Conquistata (Tasso), 45
Gibbons, Orlando, 28
Goethe, J. W. von, 230, 244
Gorges, Mrs., 125
Grotius, Hugo, 43

Hamlet, 24, 243
Hampden, John, 171
Hayley, William, 251
Hazlitt, William, 253
Hippolytus, 245
History of Britain, 78
Homer, 77, 82, 84, 89, 152, 153, 155, 171, 230
Horace, 69
Horton, 37, 40, 41, 42, 111
Hume, Patrick, 250

Iliad, The, 154, 155, 157, 162
Imitation, The, of Christ, 147–8
Indemnity, Act of, 72, 73, 74
Independent Army, The, 55, 56
Italian travels, 43–6

James I, 58
Jebb, Prof., 242–3
Job, Book of, 21, 82
Johnson, Dr. Samuel, 125, 126, 160, 162, 175, 194, 196, 206, 207, 227, 252, 253
Jones, Inigo, 16, 114
Jonson, Ben, 114, 115

Keats, John, 79, 90, 102, 110, 125, 253
Keightley, Thomas, 251
King, Edward, 42, 91, 124, 125, 127, 128–31

Landor, Walter Savage, 132
Lawes, Henry, 41, 82, 91, 116, 119
Lawrence, Henry, 69–70, 133
Lectures on the English Poets, 253
Lee, Sir Sidney, 252
Letters of State, 252
Lives of Milton, 251, 252, 253
Lives of the Poets, 252
London, 25, 49; fire of, 75

Long Parliament, 47, 63, 64, 171
Lycidas, 13, 41, 42, 90, 91, 100, 106, 123 *et sqq.*

Mackail, J. W., 94–5, 206, 211
Manso, Giovanni, 45
Marini, 45
Marlowe, Christopher, 107
Marvell, Andrew, 69, 73
Massacres in Piedmont, sonnets on, 68, 133, 139, 140–1
Masson, D., 24, 52, 68, 73, 75, 251
Medea, The, 245
Milton, 253
Milton's Prosody, 224, 253
Milton's relations :—
    Daughters, 11, 54, 69, 75–77, 218
    Deborah, 77–8
    Father, 27, 29, 37, 38–40, 42, 43, 49, 54, 75
    Infant son, 76
    Mother, 40
    Nephews, 46, 54, 61, 70, 252
    Wives—
        First, *see* Powell, Mary.
        Second, 54, 69, 71
        Third, 54
Mitford, John, 252
Monk, General, 72
Morley, Thomas, 28
Morrice, —, 72
Morus, 69

Napoleon, 9, 139
Newbolt, Henry, 120
Newton, Thomas, 251

Ode on the Nativity, 35–6, 37, 91, 93–4, 97, 98–103
Odyssey, The, 162, 196
Œdipus Coloneus, 237, 248
Œdipus Tyrannus, 233, 238, 243
On Attaining the Age of Twenty-three, sonnet, 91, 133
On His Blindness, sonnet, 62–3, 133
On the Death of a Fair Infant, 35, 97–9
Orations, 34–5
Othello, 150
Ovid, 33, 77, 124

Pamphlets, 49, 56, 69, 71
Paradise Lost, 13, 24, 25, 28, 44, 47, 55, 71, 78, 79, 80, 82, 88, 89, 90, 94, 95, 97, 101, 104, 106, 112, 113, 118, 120, 123, 125, 137, 142 *et sqq.*, 196, 197 *et sqq.*, 239, 240, 247, 248, 250, 251, 253

Paradise Regained, 13, 24, 44, 78, 167, 196 *et sqq.*, 227, 248, 250, 251
Passion, The, 103
Pattison, Mark, 131, 132, 197, 252
Penseroso, Il, 41, 70, 93, 100, 106 *et sqq.*, 239
Persæ, The, 245
Petrarch, 33, 134, 135
Phillips, Edward, 252
Pickering, William, 252
Pindar, 117
Plato, 8, 9–10, 21, 111, 156
Pleasure Reconciled to Virtue, 115
Poems, editions of, 250–1, 252
Poetical Works, The, of Mr. John Milton, 250
Pope, A., 85, 90, 91, 105, 222, 223
Portraits, 252
Powell family, 50, 53
Powell, Mary, 50–4, 69, 71
Prelude, The, 136, 228–9
Pro Populo Anglicano Defensio, 60, 61
Prometheus the Fire-Giver, 246
Prometheus Unbound, 102
Prometheus Vinctus, 21, 243, 245
Prose Works, 47 *et sqq.*, 251–2
Psalms, the, 139–40; paraphrases of, 95
Purcell, Henry, 16
Pym, John, 171

Raleigh, Sir Walter, 198, 253
Ranelagh, Lady, 69
Ready and Easy Way A, to Establish a Free Commonwealth, 65
Reason, The, of Church Government, 13, 37
Regicides, the, 55, 63, 71, 74
Reynolds, Sir Joshua, 16
Rome, 44, 209
Rossetti, Dante G., 135

St. Brides', Fleet Street, 46
St. Giles' Church, Cripplegate, 79
St. John, J. A., 252
St. Paul, 9, 144, 218
St. Paul's Cathedral, 89, 193
Salmasius, 59–62, 69, 218
Samson Agonistes, 13, 20, 24, 78, 83, 99, 199, 219 *et sqq.*, 250
Sansovino's Library, Venice, 193
Saumaise, *see* Salmasius.
Scudamore, Lord, 43

Shakspeare, W., 9, 14, 17, 32, 35, 36, 80, 85, 90, 103, 114, 118, 145, 166, 247; sonnets, 133–5, 253
Shelley, P. B., 20, 29, 50, 79, 90, 99, 102, 111, 125, 228
Shelley, Mrs. P. B., 50
Sidney, Sir Philip, 58, 98, 124, 135
Skinner, Cyriack, 62, 133
Smithfield, 72
Song on May Morning, 36, 107
Sonnets, 47, 54, 62–3, 68, 69, 91, 106, 131 *et sqq.*
Sophocles, 82, 233, 245
Spectator, The, 253
Spenser, Edmund, 93, 97, 98, 111, 115, 116, 124, 125, 153
State, The, of Innocence, 240, 253
Statius, 157
Strafford, Earl of, 171
Sumner, Rev. C. R., 252
Symmons, Charles, 252

Tasso, Torquato, 45, 82, 153, 154
Tennyson, Alfred, 69, 90, 197
Tenure of Kings and Magistrates, 56, 58, 75
Theocritus, 124
Todd, Rev. H. J., 251
Toland, John, 251
Tonson, Jacob, 250
Treatise of Christian Doctrine, 252
Trinity College Library, 89, 250
Turner, J. W. M., 16
Tyburn, 71, 90

Verrall, A. W., 240
Virgil, 82, 84, 89, 91, 124, 139, 150, 152, 153, 155, 157, 163, 175
Vita Nuova, La, 120

Waller, Edmund, 104
Warton, Joseph, 118, 126, 214
Warton, Thomas, 253
Whitehall, 58, 70, 74, 219
Williamson, Dr. G. C., 252
Winchester, Marchioness of, 36
Windsor, 37
Windsor Castle, 40
Wood, Anthony à, 31, 35, 252
Wordsworth, W., 26, 34, 79, 90, 131, 133, 135, 137, 140, 141, 206, 227–30; sonnets, 137–41, 253
Works, The, of John Milton, in Prose and Verse, 252
Wren, Sir Christopher, 16, 89
Wright, W. Aldis, 251

Young, Thomas, 27

Printed in Great Britain by The Riverside Press, Edinburgh

1¼.44